ENDORSEMENTS

THE DIMENSION OF VISIONS, DREAMS, TRANCES, AND supernatural visitations can become commonplace in your spiritual walk with the Lord. Journey with Adam F. Thompson in this book as he takes you on a marvelous journey into discovering the immeasurable world of the supernatural kingdom of God. His personal testimonies will encourage your faith and even possibly stir your spirit to receive the same type of miraculous vision in your life. In this book, Adam F. Thompson highlights the basic requirements and outlines revelatory principles that will teach you how God can use your imagination to release heaven on earth! You can hear God and you can know His direction for your life; you can decree His prophetic Word into existence; you can live in these unconstrained realms of blessing while unearthing the supernatural man! This book is powerful, a superb spiritual activator. I believe you will receive an impartation as you read!

REV. JOSHUA S. MILLS
Conference speaker and bestselling author,
31 Days to a Miracle Mindset
New Wine International Ministries
www.NewWineInternational.org

Having ministered closely with Adam for a number of years, I have personally seen him repeatedly bring the reality of heaven into a meeting and change atmospheres. Even though he has become a very close friend, I sit up and listen when he delivers God's payload from the Throne room. The words of knowledge he receives while waiting on God, and the visions he shares while ministering to people are nothing other than God-given. In this book he not only tells how it all started, but also opens his heart and shares what he personally does prior to ministry to prepare himself that he may bring Heaven to Earth. If you aspire to do the 'greater works' of Jesus-lead people to Christ, see people healed and delivered through outbreaks of the supernatural—then this book is a must read!

ADRIAN BEALE
Itinerant prophetic teacher
Co-author of *The Divinity Code to Understanding Your Dreams and Visions*

This is a faith builder book and an exciting book. Adam shows us how this supernatural realm is for everyone. He shows us how God speaks in signs and wonders and the prophetic realm.

God wants to demonstrate His power and declare His ways, not only with thunders and lightening but through His people—like you and I. The Apostle Paul said, "I come not to you with words only—but with demonstration of the Spirit and in power." The supernatural realm is where we are meant to live as Christians.

KATHIE WALTERS
Good News Ministries, Macon GA

Adam is a personal friend who has refreshed my life and the church we lead in Hong Kong. His accuracy in the gifts of God have honestly startled and thrilled me! He is so authentic that you just want to worship Jesus with relief for such Christ-centered, servant-hearted ministry. Adam has a ministry that goes to the front lines of global evangelism, willing to take risks on his very life for the purposes of God. He has a proven ministry with a solid pattern of integrity and consistency. He is an Ephesians 4 gift who empowers and equips people for supernatural ministry. Recently I had one of the most pivotal dreams in my life. Adam's interpretation of the dream was so empowering and confirming of the interpretation God had already given me that it shifted my consciousness into a higher level of confidence to boldly continue in the assignments of the Father.

This is a book that will relate instantly to the deep in you that is already calling out to the corresponding depths of the Father's pure fountains of grace toward you. Adam writes with such humor and humility that you will access the wealth of revelation this book reveals effortlessly. Get ready to go to another level. Well done, Adam! Once again you have delighted the heart of the Father and given empowerment to multitudes of people around the world with this book.

ROB RUFUS
Founding Pastor of City Church International
Hong Kong

I believe this book has been supernaturally inspired to coincide with what is a global awakening. All over the earth, the body of Christ is being awakened to the hope of their calling, the riches of their glorious inheritance and the greatness of the power toward us who believe. I believe Adam's book is a gift to the body to encourage us all to step out in our calling to walk in the supernatural power of God. *The Supernatural Man* stirs hearts to eagerly desire the greater gifts and the testimonies Adam shares impart faith to those who read them.

Adam truly is a supernatural man, known internationally as a man who ministers powerfully in the gifts of the Spirit. As part of the Australian Prophetic Council he is both a good friend and a widely respected Prophet both in Australia and internationally. I thank God for the release of this book and the blessing it will be to many.

KATHERINE RUONALA
Author of *Walking in the Miraculous—
Catching the Next Wave of Revival*
Senior Leader of the Glory City Church Network
Coordinator of the Australian Prophetic Council Reading

Adam F. Thompson's latest book, *The Supernatural Man,* was like watching a heart-wrenching, supernatural thriller on the big screen! On the edge of my seat, each story and testimony became alive and unfolded before my eyes. Better than any movie, however, this book isn't fiction, but it is jam packed with *very real* Kingdom truths and teachings—real-life stories and testimonies—that God will use to awaken the supernatural in your life. It's time for the body of Christ to wake up, get up, shake off the lethargy and fully live from *The Supernatural Man.*

ERIC GREEN
Co-founder and overseer
Kingdom Life Institute
www.kingdomlifeinstitute.com
www.ericgreen.org

I have known Adam for over twenty-five years and from a close proximity have seen him wholeheartedly pursue and lay hold of what it is to "walk in the Spirit." By cultivating a life of discipline and focus, I have seen God "show Himself strong" on Adam's behalf in many wonderful and challenging moments in his life. This book is full of testimonies and strategies that will both inspire and equip those who hunger to see God move in and through them in the power of the Holy Spirit.

TODD WEATHERLY
Field of Dreams Australia
www.fieldofdreams.org.au

DESTINY IMAGE BOOKS BY
ADAM F. THOMPSON

The Divinity Code to Understanding Your Dreams and Visions
(with Adrian Beale)

THE Supernatural
MAN

DESTINY IMAGE® PUBLISHERS, INC.

P.O. Box 310, Shippensburg, PA 17257-0310

"Promoting Inspired Lives."

This book and all other Destiny Image, Revival Press, MercyPlace, Fresh Bread, Destiny Image Fiction, and Treasure House books are available at Christian bookstores and distributors worldwide.

For a U.S. bookstore nearest you, call 1-800-722-6774.

For more information on foreign distributors, call 717-532-3040.

Reach us on the Internet: www.destinyimage.com.

ISBN 13 TP: 978-0-7684-0342-8

ISBN 13 Ebook: 978-0-7684-8495-3

For Worldwide Distribution, Printed in the U.S.A.

2 3 4 5 6 7 8 / 17 16 15

THE *Supernatural* MAN

Learn to Walk in Revelatory Realms of Heaven

ADAM F. THOMPSON

CONTENTS

Foreword

God's original design was to establish and extend His heavenly Kingdom into the realm of earth through a family of supernatural sons. The physical realm of earth was created to be an extension of God's Kingdom dominion which exists in Heaven. The Garden of Eden was designed to be Heaven on earth—the supernatural realm of Heaven expressed in the realm of the natural. However, as we know, when the fall of man occurred, man was cut off from communion with God and legal access to the supernatural realm. But, through the shed blood of Jesus Christ, we have an open door to commune with God and can access the supernatural realm of Heaven at any time.

Many leaders have boiled down Christianity to lifeless principles that have unfortunately produced a powerless, fearful, apathetic Church. Our mandate, however, is far different than what's typically communicated through a Sunday morning sermon. Jesus taught us to pray this way, *"Your kingdom come. Your will be done on earth as it is in heaven"* (Matt. 6:10). What's God's will? Heaven on earth. What's the Church's mandate? Heaven on earth. How does this happen? By cultivating the Kingdom of God in our lives through *The Supernatural Man*.

Don't look in this book for a carefully developed system of doctrinal principles—you won't find it. What you will find is a series of real-life testimonies and stories, Kingdom keys, and even impartation to unlock and crack open the realm of the supernatural in your life. Through Adam F. Thompson's book, *The Supernatural Man*, dreams, visions, prophecy, miracles, and other demonstrations of power will become part of your daily life. It's time to cast aside complacency and dead tradition, cultivate the Kingdom, and release Heaven on earth.

JEFF JANSEN
Global Fire Ministries

chapter 1

MY STORY

IN 1986, I GAVE MY LIFE TO THE LORD AND BECAME A born-again Christian. Two years later I attended a Bible college. Once I had left Bible college—and like some other students—I soon went MIA and began to backslide, simply because I had experienced information overload and not a supernatural lifestyle. In 1989, I married a beautiful woman, Paula. My life soon became entangled in the world of business, and I became a very successful businessman both financially and illustriously. I owned an advertising agency and had a partnership in a printing company; I was also a director and shareholder of a residential construction company and a finance company.

I became so engrossed in my work that I literally worked up to fifteen hours a day, six to seven days a week. The only time I was not in the office was on a Sunday morning when I would go to church to pay homage to God. On the surface it seemed as if I was a dedicated follower of the Lord, but in reality my heart had turned away from God. In Matthew 13 Jesus told the Parable of the Sower, whose seeds fell on the different paths: *"And some fell among thorns, and the thorns sprang up and choked them"* (Matt. 13:7). The thorns were indicative of the deceitfulness of riches, and this became my thorn; I was enticed and intertwined in the business world.

In 1998, I came to a place in my life where the darkness of depression started to envelop me. I began to have problems with my employees, and sticky situations arose which I could not even begin to know how to handle. Relationships started to crumble all around me, and even my relationship with my wife started to corrode and was on the verge of a breakdown. In November of that year, on a Monday night at 11:00, I came home late from work—again. My family was fast asleep, and in a bid to wind down I decided to watch CNN. Those days in Australia it was a bit of a status symbol to have CNN as one of the channels on your television. I was watching a news report of a television evangelist who had fallen and was caught making out with prostitutes. He had actually fallen and been caught in the '80s already, and now he had been caught a second time. Although it had not made the Australian news it did air on CNN. His activities left him prime game for being slaughtered by the media.

In my self-righteous manner, I started to become very angry; my heart harbored a lot of resentment and I started to turn against God. I remember asking God where He was when men like this were mocking Him. I started to shout, "Where are you God? Lord, where are you? These men are mocking you! They're making a spectacle of you and misrepresenting you. Where are you when these things happen?" Yelling even louder I repeated, "Lord, where are you when these things happen? Where are you when these people mock you?" In disgust I switched off the television and threw the remote control on the couch. Looking back, I realize I had no right to judge these men of God; I was acting with a self-righteous attitude, and my own life was a train wreck.

I came to a place in my life where the darkness of depression started to envelop me.

I lay down on the couch, and just as I started to doze off I was startled by a banging sound. I got up and walked down to the kitchen area calling out, "Hello?" as I thought that maybe one of the kids had gotten up. There was no answer and no one was walking around; the whole family was still fast asleep. I returned to the living room, intending to lie down on the couch again, when all of a sudden I began to shake. I started to feel the intense presence of God, and it was getting stronger. My whole body was literally shaking and I started to hyperventilate. The presence of God increased and increased and it became so thick in the room that it drove me down onto my knees, still shaking intensely. The pressure upon my body was so powerful I thought that I was going to die and this was the last day of my life.

The pressure increased even more and I plummeted to the ground, lying prostrate and face down on the floor. I became so overwhelmed that all I could do was start to repent for the sin in my life. The fear of the living God came upon me, and His presence was so intense that it seemed as if someone had turned baseball stadium lights on in the room. The lights were so bright and came on so suddenly that I freaked out, but I couldn't do anything except continuously repent as the Lord kept revealing my sins. One of them took me by surprise and became very confronting—it was the horoscopes. Sunday mornings I used to read the horoscopes or stars on the back of the *Sunday Mail* newspaper. Gasping and panting, I kept repenting until I started to calm down and peace began to encase my body. I still couldn't move my head and my body seemed to be frozen to the floor, but this glorious light continued to illuminate me.

As my face was down to the floor all I could do was move my eyes, and I looked upward as something caught my attention. I didn't see any particular person, but I did see the flickering of a burning fire about two meters away from me. As I focused on the fire, I sensed there was someone standing inside it and I knew it was the Lord. Tears started coming from my eyes, yet I wasn't crying. Later on, a wet patch was left on the carpet from these tears. A voice went through my spirit and said, "Well, I'm here for you now. What would you like me to do for you?" Ironically, ten minutes earlier I had been shouting at God asking Him where He was, and now He was standing right before me. I knew it was the Lord; the atmosphere was pure and righteous.

> *The fear of the living God came upon me, and His presence was so intense that it seemed as if someone had turned baseball stadium lights on in the room.*

As this voice went through me I thought that I could ask for more money, but then I realized that money was not making me happy and I was already quite well off. My marriage, however, was a mess and things weren't working out the way I had planned, so I just said, "Lord, I want wisdom." I kept saying, "Give me wisdom. Give me wisdom," over and over again until at one point I started yelling it out and eventually I shouted, "In fact, give me a double portion of King Solomon's wisdom!" As the words left my mouth everything switched off and the Lord disappeared. It seemed as if I was snapped back into reality, although I was still hyperventilating. I thought to myself, "He's gone! Did I ask for the wrong thing?"

This experience left me confused— actually I was freaked out. I ran to the bedroom to wake up Paula and I tried to explain to her that God was in the living room. Needless to say she was not pleased at being woken up in the middle of the night, let alone being woken up to the ramblings of a man professing to have seen God. I ran out of the bedroom and headed for the den to search for my Bible. Items went flying as I knocked things over until I finally found it. I opened it up and just started reading; I continued to read until I came to Second Chronicles:

> *Then God said to Solomon: "Because this was in your heart, and you have not asked riches or wealth or honor or the life of your enemies, nor have you asked long life—but have asked wisdom and knowledge for yourself, that you may judge My people over whom I have made you king— wisdom and knowledge are granted to you..."* (2 Chronicles 1:11-12).

I dropped the Bible and began to sob; I had just experienced an incredible impartation that night.

chapter 2

SUPERNATURAL
WISDOM

PAULA WAS IN THE KITCHEN THE NEXT DAY AND I KEPT pacing back and forth behind her. I was so hyped up over the experience, and I said, "Honey, the Lord has given me wisdom!" I was a bit carnal in my behavior over the experience; self-importance rose up inside of me—the Lord had stood in front of *me* and gave *me* wisdom like King Solomon. I continued speaking, "Honey, do you know what this means? This is big!" Paula just continued to ignore me, but again I said, "God has given *me* wisdom!" Paula did not respond, as you can well believe—our marriage was in trouble and here I was walking around proclaiming that I had been given wisdom like King Solomon.

I went to work with a new posture and pride filled me; I gathered all of my employees and said, "Okay everybody, I want your attention. God appeared to me last night and He gave me wisdom!" If only you could have seen the looks on their faces; they believed I had gone mad. I repeated, "God gave me wisdom, and I want you to write it down. God gave me wisdom." As the saying goes, my employees thought my cheese had slipped off my cracker and I was now officially a mental case.

For a couple of weeks thereafter, I was making the dumbest decisions I could have ever made. The staff started mocking me and kept saying, "Wow, wisdom huh?" This brought me to a place where I kept thinking "God, I believe you spoke to me; what's going on?" I was fast becoming like one of those guys from the movie *Dumb and Dumber*. Literally, I became worse in my decision making as time progressed.

Six months later, I really started pursuing God and crying out to Him. I wanted God to come back; I wanted Him to speak to me; I wanted breakthrough. Now, I believe that we already have the breakthrough out of the revelatory realm; we can step into that breakthrough as it already happened through the finished work of the cross. During this period, however, I had a lack of doctrine and I just kept crying out, "Lord, I want you to bless me; I want a breakthrough." I went into the den, lay on the floor, held onto the table leg, and out of sheer desperation I just said to the Lord, "I'm not going to let go of this leg until you bless me." I was crying out to such a point that after a few hours God honored my plea and something supernaturally hit me and extreme joy just came over me.

> *I really started pursuing God and crying out to Him. I wanted God to come back; I wanted Him to speak to me; I wanted breakthrough.*

The joy was so incredible. It was a baptism I had not experienced before. I was swathed in a joy of tongues that literally left me rolling on the floor for hours every time I went into the den. I didn't know what was happening to me and neither did Paula—the power of God just came so strongly that I experienced uncontrollable laughter under the anointing. Later, I learned about Rodney Howard-Browne and the Toronto movement where people were experiencing this same type of anointing. I originally believed that this phenomenon was caused by the location of my den; I had no idea that this type of anointing was happening in other parts of the world. I then realized that God can manifest in certain locations, but He can also manifest upon you anywhere and at any given time. All you have to do to experience God's manifested presence is to call upon His name and worship Him in spirit and in truth, as spoken by Jesus when He was at the well with the Samaritan woman:

> *But the hour is coming, and now is, when the true worshipers will worship the Father in spirit and truth; for the Father is seeking such to worship*

*Him. God is Spirit, and those who worship Him
must worship in spirit and truth* (John 4:23-24).

I used to say to Paula, "If you go into that room you will
fall over and laugh for an hour or so."

She always replied with, "I'm not going in there!" As time
progressed the laughter continued, and when Paula had girl
friends over for coffee all they could hear was this sound like
a psychotic carnival clown laughing his head off in the den. It
raised a lot of concern and many questions as to what was happening. Embarrassed, Paula would avoid the conversation and
reply with, "Ummm, nothing!" Paula stayed well away from the
den when I was in there. Who could blame her? This was a new
experience for her.

I learned that before Heidi Baker went to Toronto she
really labored in her ministry, but once she got to Toronto
she got whacked in the Holy Ghost. I was told that she was
pushed around in a wheelchair for a whole week because she
could not stand under the power and anointing of God. She
went through a transformation that could not be denied—she
planted thousands of churches after that. It was a great testament to God's glory; there was real fruit from that experience.
Now, I was going through a similar experience where I couldn't
stop laughing or speaking in tongues.

Afterward, when I had a debriefing session with the Lord,
I realized that when He gave me wisdom it was wisdom from

above and not a natural or worldly wisdom. I thought I was going to become an intellectual genius, but I was given a supernatural wisdom. Jesus said in Luke:

> *The queen of the South will rise up in the judgment with the men of this generation and condemn them, for she came from the ends of the earth to hear the wisdom of Solomon; and indeed a greater than Solomon is here* (Luke 11:31).

Jesus was talking about Himself, and I believe that when we are baptized and completely saturated and transformed in His presence, the one greater than Solomon is in all of us and He gives us wisdom and revelation knowledge.

> *I thought I was going to become an intellectual genius, but I was given a supernatural wisdom.*

It was a very interesting time of discovery for me, as I had no idea that God would give me the gift to interpret dreams and visions. In the book of Daniel it says:

> *...God gave them knowledge and skill in all literature and wisdom; and Daniel had understanding in all visions and dreams. Now at the end of the days, when the king had said that they should be brought in, the chief of the eunuchs brought them in before Nebuchadnezzar. Then the king*

> *interviewed them, and among them all none
> was found like Daniel, Hananiah, Mishael, and
> Azariah; therefore they served before the king. And
> in all matters of wisdom and understanding about
> which the king examined them, he found them ten
> times better than all the magicians and astrologers
> who were in all his realm* (Daniel 1:17-20).

Daniel had the wisdom to understand the mysteries of Heaven.

In Acts, Stephen talks about Joseph being a dream interpreter who stood before Pharaoh with great favor and wisdom. God *"...gave him favor and wisdom in the presence of Pharaoh, king of Egypt..."* (Acts 7:10). This wisdom was not from this world, but it was a supernatural wisdom given to understand the mysteries of God, to tap into the revelatory realm, and to grasp the realities of Heaven.

We can also have this wisdom today. A part of this revelation is knowing who you are and how your identity is in Jesus Christ. That is part of the wisdom and knowledge—Christ in us, the hope of glory (see Col. 1:27). Meditate on John 17 for a greater understanding of this fact.

chapter 3

LIVING FOR GOD

AFTER THIS SUPERNATURAL TRANSACTION HAD occurred, I started to move in the gifts and began working out my prophetic calling. I was in a new period of growth where I just could not stop speaking in tongues. The baptism of the Holy Spirit and speaking in tongues came so powerfully that it became the reality of my existence. There is so much controversy in Christianity when it comes to speaking in tongues, and I believe this is because the enemy wants to cloud and confuse this gift. He is terrified of believers laying claim to it and living it out.

God can diversify the tongues from one Spirit—the Holy Spirit. First Corinthians says, *"He who speaks in a tongue edifies himself, but he who prophesies edifies the church"* (1 Cor. 14:4). There are tongues for self-edification which can be used for as long as you like.

There are also tongues for public assembly. These tongues are used for interpretation of prophecies as are most commonly experienced in Pentecostal churches.

> *How is it then, brethren? Whenever you come together, each of you has a psalm, has a teaching, has a tongue, has a revelation, has an interpretation. Let all things be done for edification* (1 Corinthians 14:26).

**There is so much controversy in Christianity
when it comes to speaking in tongues,
and I believe this is because the enemy
wants to cloud and confuse this gift.
He is terrified of believers laying
claim to it and living it out.**

There are tongues for intercession:

> *Likewise the Spirit also helps in our weaknesses. For we do not know what we should pray for as we ought, but the Spirit Himself makes intercession for us with groanings which cannot be uttered. Now He who searches the hearts knows what the mind of the Spirit is, because He makes intercession for the saints according to the will of God* (Romans 8:26-27).

Intercession can be for yourself or for others. Tongues can be used as a sign to the unbeliever; someone may start speaking in tongues while they are ministering or preaching and speak in a perfect dialect of a language that they have no knowledge of but someone in the meeting has a clear understanding of what is being said. I have actually experienced this; when I was in Seattle I kept saying "Ramah Sukkah" over and over again all the time while travelling to Florida. In a Messianic church, a Jewish lady came up to me and asked if I realized what I was saying. I did not know, and she explained that *Ramah Sukkah* in the Hebrew language meant that I was in a tabernacle in a booth in a high place. This was a sign to her that all which we had preached was indeed the truth.

I wanted the perfect will of God in my life, and I had such a revelation of what it means to speak in tongues that I actually stopped working in all of my businesses to just go and speak in tongues. This is not a formula or a must-do for others. I was fortunate to have the right management team in place to oversee the businesses; because of them, I could afford to just walk away. For two years I walked the streets, speaking in tongues for six hours a day, five days a week. I was so passionate about serving God; I had had enough of serving myself and I just wanted God's perfect will manifested in my life, so it was quite easy for me to just pray in tongues continuously. In hindsight, I would have done things a bit differently. I lacked wisdom in my dealings and social interactions; I gave no thought to other people's reactions. Imagine the poor checkout people in the shopping centers having this strange man in front of them speaking another language. They must have thought I was mad.

I ask you this question: "Do you want the perfect will of God in your life?" Most of you would reply with a resounding *yes*. I suggest you start speaking in tongues. At first it will begin as self-edification, but it will quickly diversify into intercession for your life, as we read above in Romans 8 where the Holy Spirit intercedes on your behalf. This is a perfect prayer—the Holy Spirit praying on your behalf directly to your heavenly Father. Soon the obstacles of your life will begin to be removed and you will be transformed until you are in the center of God's perfect will.

> *For two years I walked the streets, speaking in tongues for six hours a day, five days a week.*

I myself am a work in progress. I'm not saying you have to pray in tongues six hours a day—this is not a formula, it's what worked for me. I'm the type of person who just throws himself into something and goes all out. I have seen how people I have mentored experience change and transformation in their lives by praying in the Holy Ghost one to two hours a day. A lot of people spend their time driving around every day—this is the most opportune time to be alone and praying in tongues.

It says in the Bible that your mind is unfruitful when you speak in tongues, so you can listen to teachings or worship music or just soak in the presence of God. You will find that if you speak in tongues for at least one to two hours a day, in about three months you will start to sense and see things beginning to shift in your life and in your spirit man. God will start to unveil revelation; this is called walking in the spirit. This has changed my life.

I want to brag a bit about what God has done in my life in the past ten years (see Gal. 6:14). I am the co-author of *The Divinity Code to Understanding Your Dreams and Visions*, written with my good friend Adrian Beale. The book is becoming a bestseller and has made it to number one on Amazon's list of Pentecostal books. We are really blessed by what God has done; I would never have thought of this happening in the natural, but God has brought me into this destiny. Adrian and I have been doing conferences around the world, equipping the body of Christ to hear the voice of God through visions and dreams, moving in the supernatural realm, and walking as Jesus walked, as it says in First John: *"He who says he abides in Him ought himself also to walk just as He walked"* (1 John 2:6).

Equipping the saints is not the be-all and end-all of our destiny. The one thing I have loved doing the most for the past ten years is mission trips—going to underdeveloped countries, taking the gospel to tough areas, doing crusades, and seeing many thousands of decisions for Christ. I've seen many healings—I've

seen a person healed of leprosy, blind eyes opening, and crip-
ples walking. We have done feeding programs for children and
have been involved with pastors in doing pastors' conferences.
I've been on many adventures and come up against many chal-
lenges, too.

> *I've seen a person healed of leprosy, blind*
> *eyes opening, and cripples walking.*

I have preached and seen hundreds of people turn to Christ
in Pakistan. I have sailed through the islands of the Philippines
on the Gospel Cruise with Todd Weatherly to preach the gospel. We came against typhoons, we were stranded at sea, we
walked through snake and sea urchin-infested waters, and we
had to carry our suitcases above our heads in order to get to the
places we needed to preach! I have been bitten by fire ants, and
I've come up against terrorists. I have encountered all of this
for the sake of the gospel. The Holy Spirit has given me the
strength to do this, and I hope He will use this book to inspire
you to do more. In the natural, I would never have thought
I would be doing this, but I am fulfilling God's perfect will
today. I encourage you to seek God, pray in tongues, and let His
Spirit unfold His perfect will for your life.

chapter 4

VISIONS AND DREAMS

WHETHER YOU HAVE VISIONS AND DREAMS NOW OR YOU do not have any at all or are not aware that God speaks this way, I want you to be aware that this is a very important part of cultivating the Kingdom of Heaven, especially in the last days. The prophet Joel prophesied:

> *And it shall come to pass afterward that I will pour out My Spirit on all flesh; your sons and your daughters shall prophesy, your old men shall dream dreams, your young men shall see visions* (Joel 2:28).

That prophecy was fulfilled in Acts 2:17, which was the birthing of the New Covenant era. It was a major event when it came to God's plan; He made an incredible change to planet

Earth and to His fulfilling of the Old Covenant. He achieved it through Jesus Christ being raised from the dead and going to the Father. Jesus said to His disciples, *"A little while, and you will not see Me; and again a little while, and you will see Me, because I go to the Father"* (John 16:16). This was not the second coming of Jesus; He came in the form of an outpouring of His power and authority through the Holy Spirit to equip us. The apostle Peter gave one of his best sermons on record in Acts 2 when he quoted the prophet Joel.

In the New Testament, when Jesus was with Peter we see that Peter stumbled, but when we read about him in the Book of Acts we see how the Holy Spirit completely transformed Peter into a different man. He became a man of boldness, a supernatural man who had visions and performed miracles in Jesus's name. The apostle Paul also operated in this realm; both of them went into trances and they operated in the seer realm and the realm of revelation through visions.

Jesus called some of His disciples "Sons of Thunder" as they were "men of the flesh":

> *Simon, to whom He gave the name Peter; James the son of Zebedee and John the brother of James, to whom He gave the name Boanerges, that is, "Sons of Thunder..."* (Mark 3:16-17).

These were rough-hewn guys—amazing, colorful characters who would not back away from a confrontation. In fact, they might even have looked forward to one. They could be very aggressive and at times very insensitive. On one occasion, when the people in a village of Samaria were not responsive to the message of Jesus, it was James and John who wanted to call down fire from Heaven on them:

> *And when His disciples James and John saw this, they said, "Lord, do You want us to command fire to come down from heaven and consume them, just as Elijah did?"* (Luke 9:54)

He came in the form of an outpouring of His power and authority through the Holy Spirit to equip us.

When Jesus spoke of His own impending death—about how He would be betrayed and then handed over to the Gentiles to be mocked, spit upon, scourged, and ultimately killed—James and John blurted out:

> *Teacher, we want You to do for us whatever we ask. ...Grant us that we may sit, one on Your right hand and the other on Your left, in Your glory* (Mark 10:35,37).

Was that a good time to bring this up? It would be like saying, "Really? Could I have your car?" to someone who just found out they had one week to live. These guys just said what they thought.

And they were just like us—hopelessly human and remarkably unremarkable. Jesus called them because He knew who they were before the foundations of the earth and He knew the will of the Father for them. So, too, can we be transformed as disciples of Christ and experience this realm of operating in visions and dreams, for it is our Father's will to operate out of Heaven.

In these last days, signs, wonders, miracles, and receiving dreams and visions are scriptural for the saints corporately to move in. Dreams and visions alone are not the goal—some people have accused me of being a horoscope reader and other crazy things—but dreams and visions are very scriptural. They are a way of communicating with God through the Holy Spirit. Dreams and visions are only a means to an end; the end in itself is Jesus Christ and the revelation of His death and resurrection. Dreams, visions, signs, and wonders are only the pointers to God. They are not to be the focal point—Jesus is the focal point, and having an intimate relationship with Him is what we strive for. The one great miracle, sign, and wonder that many people don't recognize is someone coming out of the darkness and being transformed into a son of the Kingdom of Heaven.

> *Giving thanks to the Father who has qualified us to be partakers of the inheritance of the saints in the light. He has delivered us from the power of darkness and conveyed us into the kingdom of the Son of His love, in whom we have redemption through His blood, the forgiveness of sins* (Colossians 1:12-14).

Dreams, visions, signs, and wonders are only the pointers to God. They are not to be the focal point—Jesus is the focal point, and having an intimate relationship with Him is what we strive for.

This is an amazing miracle—a person coming out of a train-wrecked life and being transformed into the likeness of Christ, looking like a disciple, and becoming that sign and wonder who reflects the King of Glory. Without this miracle occurring, all of the other signs, wonders, dreams, and visions are just party tricks. There are people who move in the prophetic, in healings, and in words of knowledge but their lives are a mess; their gifts do not qualify them as being a disciple of Christ. To qualify as a disciple of Christ is to reflect His glory and allow the hope of glory, Christ in us, to be magnified and ooze out of our whole being.

PREPARING TO RECEIVE VISIONS AND DREAMS

I want to use this opportunity to coach you on how to position yourself to activate and receive visions and dreams. As saints we have the ability to do this—to hear from God through visions and dreams.

We are made up of three components—spirit, body, and soul. The brain is part of the body; it is the flesh or the hardware. The mind is part of the soul realm, and this is the seat of our emotions and will and is similar to a computer's operating system, directing our actions. I believe the subconscious mind is where our spirit man resides. No one really knows where our subconscious mind is located; some people say it is in the back of our heads, others say it is in the spinal column, I believe from experience it is in the center of your solar plexus area. When you sleep your brain is resting—your mind shuts down and goes into sleep mode, but your subconscious mind becomes quite active. It is during this sleep time that you dream. You do not have control over your dreams, and this is when the subconscious mind taps into the everlasting doors (see Ps. 24:7). This is an eternal realm you are zoning into; it is like going into a trance.

> *To qualify as a disciple of Christ is to reflect His glory and allow the hope of glory, Christ in us, to be magnified and ooze out of our whole being.*

When you are in that sleep state, the subconscious mind is being ministered to by the Holy Spirit. It also opens us up to the heavenlies where ministering angels can interact with us. However, for unbelievers or Christians robbed by lies out of ignorance, this can also open them up to being tormented by demon powers. This is not to say that you are possessed by demons, but that they can influence your dreams. You may have heard the saying, "The darkest hour is just before the dawn." This is when the demonic realm is also active and usually occurs during the third watch of the night. This is clearly demonstrated when Jesus was in the Garden of Gethsemane. Demonic activity was occurring in the spiritual realm. Jesus prayed three times throughout that night, and it was after the third time spent in prayer that His accusers came to arrest Him. The "night watch" is divided into four three-hour intervals—the first watch is 6 PM to 9 PM, the second is 9 PM to 12 AM, the third is 12 AM to 3 AM, and the fourth is 3 AM to 6 AM.

The six to ten hours of the night that you are sleeping is the longest period of time going without food—it is like going on a short fast. When you fast, you become very sensitive to your spirit man, and during the fourth watch of the night your dreams can become very vivid. I do fast when I am awake and I have visions when I am standing up; these are called open visions. In these visions I can receive people's names; I can see the conditions of their lives and any sicknesses in their bodies. This happens often in conferences. When I hold a person's hand, I can receive an open vision. I remember one time in Australia I called out the name of the child of the mother whose hand I was holding, and I saw in a vision that the child was being tormented. After praying for the child I was told the child had Asperger's. After that they received a dramatic turnaround and healing for the whole family.

When I fast and read the Word, I am able to tap into that zone. I open myself up to the Word of God, which divides soul and spirit (see Heb. 4:12). When I fast I become more sensitive to my spirit man, which helps me to identify my soulish desires and allows me to be open to what the Holy Spirit is saying to my spirit man. Some grace teachers tell us that you do not need to fast anymore, and though I agree in a sense, I still fast. I believe that we do not need to fast like people in the Old Testament who worked themselves up and fasted when they needed breakthroughs. We already have the breakthrough; when Jesus died and rose again we received our breakthroughs. All we need to do now is have faith. Faith activates our spirits and gives us the ability to enter into that manifestation of the breakthrough.

When I was young in the Lord I used to take on big fasts. Once I said to myself that I was not going to eat until I saw Jesus face to face. I was so passionate about it, and I believed that if I fasted Jesus would come and speak to me. After 20 days, I hadn't eaten a thing; I kept asking the Lord to reveal Himself to me. I was the director of a building company at that time, and I remember going into the monthly board meeting. My uncle, who was the managing director, turned to me in front of all the other board members and said, "Adam, you look terrible! What have you been doing?" I looked like a deer caught in the headlights. I replied that I was fasting; I was not going to eat until I saw Jesus face to face and He talked to me.

My uncle gave me a stern look and said, "You know, that will do it! If you don't eat, you will see Jesus—that's a given!"

All of the other members started to laugh at me. It was so true; I was on a quick way to starving myself to death. There are people who fast for 40 days at a time, but in these cases they are lead by the Holy Spirit and He sustains them through these fasts. I still fast, but now I am more sensitive to the leading of the Holy Spirit when I begin and end my fasts. Fasting is a key to activating your spirit man to receive visions and dreams.

> *"You know, that will do it! If you don't eat, you will see Jesus—that's a given!"*

Worship is another key to activating the Kingdom of Heaven. Being intimate with the Lord, who is the lover of your soul, is fundamental in walking in the spirit. When you worship in spirit and truth it leads you into a place of soaking where you have full access to the throne room of grace and have full intimacy with the Lord. This is where your heart touches the very heart of God and you can just rest in His embrace, let His perfect peace and presence surround you and cloak you. Soaking is one aspect of opening your spirit man to receive the impartation of visions and dreams.

Have you ever come home at the end of a busy day, lay down on the bed, and while worshiping God found yourself on the edge of falling asleep, half asleep and half awake? Medical terminology calls this experience the theta state of sleep but the Bible calls this a trance. You are not totally asleep nor are you totally awake. Once you enter into that place of rest, images start rushing through your mind. This is actually you having a vision. You need to discipline yourself to come out of that state and write down what you have seen. These images can be symbolic—God is speaking to you in a riddle or abstractedly. You may question the scriptural basis for this, or you may fear that this is not of God or is dangerous, but in Acts 10 Peter experienced this type of vision through a trance-like state:

> *The next day, as they went on their journey and drew near the city, Peter went up on the housetop to pray, about the sixth hour. Then he became very hungry and wanted to eat; but while they made ready, he fell into a trance and saw heaven opened and an object like a great sheet bound at the four corners, descending to him and let down to the earth. In it were all kinds of four-footed animals of the earth, wild beasts, creeping things, and birds of the air. And a voice came to him, "Rise, Peter; kill and eat." But Peter said, "Not so, Lord! For I have never eaten anything common or unclean." And a voice spoke to him again the second time, "What God has cleansed you must not call common." This*

was done three times. And the object was taken up into heaven again (Acts 10:9-16).

> *This is where your heart touches the very heart of God and you can just rest in His embrace, let His perfect peace and presence surround you and cloak you.*

When Peter came out of this trance he needed an interpretation of its meaning, and God spoke to him, telling him to go with the men who were at the door for he was called to go and preach to the Gentiles.

In Acts 22, Paul fell into a trance and the Lord spoke to him and gave him a word. *"Now it happened, when I returned to Jerusalem and was praying in the temple, that I was in a trance"* (Acts 22:17). God can speak to us by this means; it is scriptural and is clearly written in the Bible.

Have you ever been in a situation where you have fallen into a trance or have entered into a sleep mode and you start seeing images that seem to flash before you? In this moment, God is speaking to your spirit man, and in this state everything seems to make sense—your spirit man is agreeing to what is happening. When you snap out of it and think about the vision or dream, however, all of a sudden you start thinking that it was crazy, that it made no sense at all. When you were in the trance or near-sleep state it seemed to make perfect sense, but now when you are awake it makes no sense at all. The reason why this happens is that when you are in a trance or entering into that sleep mode your spirit man is agreeing with the things of Heaven; it is bearing witness to the events of that eternal realm. This is where you come from—the Kingdom of Heaven—so you actually start to understand the mysteries of God. But when you come out of it, those images filter into your carnal mind and they may not make any sense. This is when you will need an interpretation of those images. Your dreams are often given in the form of parables and symbols, and these most often need to be interpreted.

> *When you are in a trance or entering into that sleep mode your spirit man is agreeing with the things of Heaven; it is bearing witness to the events of that eternal realm.*

God can also speak to you clearly and directly in times of urgency. For example, God warned Joseph in a dream to flee to Egypt.

> *Now when they had departed, behold, an angel of the Lord appeared to Joseph in a dream, saying, "Arise, take the young Child and His mother, flee to Egypt, and stay there until I bring you word; for Herod will seek the young Child to destroy Him"* (Matthew 2:13).

You can have different types of dreams with different manifestations. They are not always the same, and God may speak to you through parables, metaphors, or plainly where you know exactly what He is saying.

chapter 5

IDENTITY IN CHRIST

I OFTEN WONDERED WHY GOD WOULD SPEAK TO US IN dreams and visions. God speaks to us in so many different ways; for some, hearing from God through dreams and visions is the primary way of communication. For others, God most often speaks through His Word. When you are reading the Word, it starts off as the *logos* or written word, but soon it changes into the *rhema* or living word of God and revelation starts to be released. This is the main way God speaks to me to this day—through His Word.

When Jesus walked the planet, He was one of the most powerful communicators in history. Jesus spoke through the use of symbols, images, riddles, and parables; He taught the ways of the Kingdom by using circumstances, environments, and the things that were familiar to people. Today, He will use elements of our home and work environments, combine them with our experiences, and use parables to communicate with us.

Our minds are very powerful. God created our minds to create, and we are creative beings. He communicates through images and symbols in a powerful way. It has been shown that the mind absorbs images. For example, when we read, rather than our brains reading a sentence as separate words, our eyes scan clusters of three or four words and instantly "translate" their shapes into meaning. Your brain doesn't "sound out" the letters but *recognizes* the distinctive shape or image of the word and assigns it a meaning.

When I was a child I had dyslexia and struggled to read, but since accepting the Lord He changed my mind. Now I absorb the words through symbols and imagery and it has become easier to read and write. Images are used everywhere; they are commonly used in marketing campaigns and are seen all around us—from the signs on the roads to the packaging on foods. If you see a roadway crossing sign, you will notice an image of a mother holding a child's hand and know immediately you need to be aware of people crossing the road. The image registers before the words written underneath it. Another use of images is on computers. The icons have universal meanings, and people recognize the images before they read the words associated with them.

Our minds are very powerful. God created our minds to create, and we are creative beings.

God speaks to us in dreams and visions through the use of symbols and images, and these help us to remember the dream upon waking up. We do not always recall the dream, but most often we can replay it in our mind thanks to the pictures stored within. Jesus spoke to His disciples in parables. Parables were like dreams—He used life symbols to communicate with the people. For example, when He spoke to the fishermen He told them they would be *fishers of men.* To farmers He spoke of *sowing* and *reaping,* and to the businessman He spoke of *talents.* The disciples needed a reference point to understand the meaning of Jesus's teachings, and this began with parables. Just as a baby learns by identifying pictures first and from there the words start to flow, so too do we drink the milk before we can chew the meat (see 1 Cor. 3:2).

The Lord still speaks to us in parables through our dreams. You may wonder why God doesn't speak to us plainly and directly. There is a Scripture which says, *"It is the glory of God to conceal a matter, but the glory of kings is to search out a matter"* (Prov. 25:2). God wants us to seek Him out, just like the Scriptures state: *"But seek first the kingdom of God and His righteousness, and all these things shall be added to you"* (Matt. 6:33). He wants us to search Him out and seek out the mysteries of Heaven. It is like in Matthew 13 when Jesus spoke about the treasure hidden in the field. You will do whatever it takes to be able to purchase that field to find that treasure, and God wants us to find Him—He wants us to exercise our spiritual senses and come into maturity of hearing and knowing Him.

> *The Lord still speaks to us in*
> *parables through our dreams.*

Once we have learned to hear the voice of God, we come out of the basic, elementary teachings and into maturity. The mysteries are no longer such, but they become revelation. In John 16, Jesus began by speaking figuratively before He spoke plainly:

> *These things I have spoken to you in figurative language; but the time is coming when I will no longer speak to you in figurative language, but I will tell you plainly about the Father* (John 16:25).

When we come into that place of revelation, we receive liberation which gives us confidence to take our inheritance and to start activating the Kingdom riches. Once we see that the Kingdom is more real than what we see with our eyes, we have the confidence to start decreeing, activating, and cultivating the Kingdom into the natural, Adamic realm.

I mentioned before that the revelation of Jesus Christ and having intimacy with Him is the most important event of our Christian walk. A part of that revelation of Jesus Christ is knowing our identity in Him. If we don't know our identity in Jesus Christ or understand who we are and what we are called to be and do, then we will be like a person lost at sea on a raft, not knowing where we are going. God doesn't want us to live like that; He wants us to know the revelation of Jesus Christ, the image of God, and His Kingdom, and that comes from knowing who we were before the foundations of the Earth—knowing who we really are in the Kingdom of Heaven. Jesus knew us before the foundations of the earth. God said to Jeremiah that He knew him before he was formed in his mother's womb, and He knew us before the foundations of the earth too.

> *When we come into that place of revelation,*
> *we receive liberation which gives us*
> *confidence to take our inheritance and to*
> *start activating the Kingdom riches.*

The following testimony impacted my life and changed the way I think and relate to God. It is written by Brannon M. Nix, the founder of Sozo Birmingham in Alabama (visit www.sozobirmingham.net). It has made me want to search God out even more:

TESTIMONY

In April 2007, I was in Jefferson County Jail in Birmingham, Alabama. I was sharing the cell with a man who knew the Lord. The whole time he was there, he would read his Bible and fast. For about two weeks, he tried to minister to me, but I would not allow him to because I didn't want anything to do with it.

This one day I was in a place of sadness and feeling down. He was reading his Bible, and something in me desired to know what he was reading, so I asked him to read something to me. He read from Psalm 23: *"You prepare a table before me in the presence of my enemies. You anoint my head with oil; my cup overflows"* (Ps. 23:5 NIV). When he got to that verse, I stopped him and asked what it means to anoint your head with oil. He took me to the Book of James:

> *Is anyone among you sick? Let them call the elders of the church to pray over them and anoint them with oil in the name of the Lord. And the prayer offered in faith will make the sick person well; the Lord will raise them up. If they have sinned, they will be forgiven* (James 5:14-15 NIV).

At that moment, I thought to myself, *That is exactly what I need. I could use some of that.* So I asked him if he could anoint me. He said, "Well, I am not an elder."

I looked at him and said, "Dude, you're old enough!"

He was around 48 years old, and he kind of laughed. I was so unchurched that I didn't even know what an elder was. Then he said, "We don't have any oil." At that moment I began to look around the jail cell, and my eyes met with my little bottle of shampoo. I picked it up and read the label on the back. It said it had oil in it! So I told my cell mate that this shampoo had oil in it and that if we prayed for it God would make it holy.

So we prayed and asked God to make the shampoo holy, and then he asked me how I wanted to go about doing this. I told him that I would read Psalm 23 and when I get to the part, *"You anoint my head with oil,"* he had to anoint me at that very second. So when he did, the power of the Holy Spirit came upon me. It was as if hot oil was being poured over my head, and it flowed all the way down to the bottom of my feet and my body trembled. I have never felt anything like that before. It freaked me out a little. Then about sixty seconds later, the cell door opened for us to go out to eat. I could no longer stay in my cell. I went out to the main area with the other inmates. I was so shaken up that I gave my food tray away. If you give your food tray away, you know it has to be a miracle with the small amount of food we are given. So I did, and I sat alone by the wall and didn't speak to anyone. Finally, around 9:00 PM they led us back into our cell.

It was as if hot oil was being poured over my head, and it flowed all the way down to the bottom of my feet and my body trembled. I have never felt anything like that before.

When I got back to my cell I read the book of Ephesians. When I had finished, I stood up and noticed that my cell mate was asleep. The cell light was turned off from the control center. It was almost too perfect to be true, and at that moment I saw a vision of my grandfather who was a Church of God pastor. He died in the '90s. When I saw the vision of him, it was as if the scales were removed from my eyes and the veil was lifted. It was as if I remembered who I was. I looked at my life of sin and it shamed me because deep within me I knew that that wasn't me. I was back in my right mind. The best way to explain it is that before I was born I knew Father God; I understood His presence in the room. I knew Him more than I knew my earthly parents. I was with Him in the beginning when He formed my spirit. He was the one I knew in that moment, and I understood and recognized His presence. And then I came alive and remembered who I was. That night, God delivered me; I quit smoking and I quit living a destructive lifestyle of drugs and life-controlling issues.

THE VISION

After my encounter of salvation, God took me into a trance. It seemed like a daydream on steroids. I was with Him before the foundation of the world. I was in my full identity as a son of God, a priest, a king, and a prophet: *"And hath made us kings and priests unto God and his Father; to him be glory and dominion forever and ever. Amen"* (Rev. 1:6 KJV).

There were no more lies; it was me and the Father in union, and I was experiencing the fullness and ecstasy of God. He was standing on my left and I was sitting on His right. Suddenly, a blue globe appeared in front of us. It looked like planet Earth. The thought came to mind that the journey to earth was ahead of me. In my mind I was wondering what was going to happen on this journey. Father God, knowing what I was thinking because He incited the whole thing, motioned to me to ask Him the question that was on my mind. God's knowing can be confirmed in Psalms:

> *You know when I sit and when I rise; you perceive my thoughts from afar. Your eyes saw my unformed body; all the days ordained for me were written in your book before one of them came to be* (Psalm 139:2,16 NIV).

There were no more lies; it was me and the Father in union, and I was experiencing the fullness and ecstasy of God.

I asked Him what was going to happen when I went there, and He answered: "You will forget who I am and who you are." In that moment, this news was devastating. He let me experience the sadness of His answer for what seemed like an eternity, then He gently continued: "But your journey in life will be to discover who I am and who you are. In other words, when you find Me you will find yourself."

> We weren't created sinners; we were born into sin, which caused us to forget who we are. And the father of lies veiled us with his lies.
>
> —Brannon M. Nix

We need to spend the rest of our lives discovering the revelatory understanding of who God is and who we are in Him through His Word. We as saints must meditate on our heavenly positions:

> *If then you were raised with Christ, seek those things which are above, where Christ is, sitting at the right hand of God. Set your mind on things above, not on things on the earth. For you died, and your life is hidden with Christ in God. When Christ who is our life appears, then you also will appear with Him in glory* (Colossians 3:1-4).

We need to spend the rest of our lives discovering the revelatory understanding of who God is and who we are in Him through His Word.

Our identity in Christ Jesus is a major essence to our Christian walk, and I encourage you to seek the Lord through His Word and through the dreams and visions He imparts to you.

chapter 6

THE HEAVENLIES

THERE ARE DIFFERENT MANIFESTATIONS OF THE VOICE of God through dreams and visions. I believe that hearing the voice of God through dreams and visions is for all Christians, not just for the prophets like in the Old Testament. In the New Covenant, all of us corporately have the ability to hear from God. It is unscriptural for a man to continuously go to a man of God or prophet to hear the Word of the Lord—those days are over. I have people who come to me wanting to hear a word from the Lord, and they can become quite demanding in wanting it. I often think to myself in these situations: "Read your Bible!" Some people are too lazy to seek God; they want a quick fix and will therefore seek out a prophet for a word. There is a time and place that the prophetic word is released. Mostly this is from the pulpit, and this is how I minister. People want to have their dreams and visions interpreted out of curiosity, like reading horoscopes or having their palms read.

If you are a dream interpreter and you are discipling someone and constantly interpreting their dreams but they are not displaying any change, growth, or fruit in their lives, then I encourage you to shut it down and stop doing it. They are using you like a fortune-teller. This is not what I and Adrian Beale are about. Dreams and visions are for equipping the body and should bear fruit. People need to grow into the understanding of the Kingdom of Heaven and the revelation of Jesus Christ. There are Christians out there who are fickle, but we love them even though they are not dedicated to a relationship with God or have substance to their lives. Often people will come to our church, Field of Dreams, and exclaim that this is the kind of church they have been looking for and sing its praises, but we never see them again.

> *People want to have their dreams and visions interpreted out of curiosity, like reading horoscopes or having their palms read.*

God can speak to you through a prophetic gifting, like when he spoke to Daniel and showed him the broader world events. God can give you warnings of situations that will arise in your city or neighborhood that will affect the larger community. God is talking to you on a larger scale of things to come; these events are often a foregone conclusion. God helped Joseph interpret Pharaoh's dreams of the impending famine. This pre-knowing is called *foretelling*. Foretelling is God revealing an unstoppable event or disaster through a dream or a vision in order to prepare you or the community.

God can also use dreams and visions to reveal His promises, which are stored up in Heaven where the full provision of God exists. Some Christians call this the third heaven, and we can activate these promises by proclaiming God's truth—in other words, *forth* telling. These promises are real and they need to be activated by faith. God wants you to exercise your faith, taking dominion, and decreeing His promises into your life: *"For all the promises of God in Him are Yes, and in Him Amen, to the glory of God through us"* (2 Cor. 1:20). God can show you these promises through dreams and visions. For example, one day I was praying with Todd Weatherly and God showed me a vision of a gold angel. I believed it was an angel of finance, and I did need some money, as I was struggling financially at the time. I said to Todd that God was about to release some finances to me and I was about to prosper because He had shown me this gold angel and the promises of Heaven. I knew I had to call this in to receive the prosperity, so I started prophesying and declaring it into being. Within a few days, I received thousands of dollars.

Once I was praying for a vehicle and God showed me a vision of a white car with an "H" on it—I thought it could be a Hyundai or a Holden. God wanted me to start taking dominion and decreeing it into the natural. This forth-telling is decreeing the promises of Heaven into your life. God was showing the promises and riches stored up in Heaven, and He wanted me to activate my faith and prophesy it into the Adamic realm. These promises are more real than what is in the natural. Within three weeks someone gave me a white Honda as a gift. Three years later, I needed another car so I started to call it in, and another person gave me a Mazda 6. I find it amazing how God operates. Symbolically, a new car can indicate a new destiny, and the name *Mazda* symbolically means "God of wisdom."

> *I knew I had to call this in to receive the*
> *prosperity, so I started prophesying and*
> *declaring it into being. Within a few*
> *days, I received thousands of dollars.*

God can give you personal warnings through dreams and visions, as seen when the magi were warned in a dream to take a different route back home in order to avoid Herod: *"Then, being divinely warned in a dream that they should not return to Herod, they departed for their own country another way"* (Matt. 2:12). This was not a foregone conclusion; these wise men could have been ignorant of the warning and returned to Herod, but they trusted in the warning dream. You can also have dreams where your spirit man taps into the second heaven. This is where your spirit man is like a transistor radio and becomes very sensitive to what is happening in the heavenlies. These dreams can seem more like nightmares, but God is communicating to you by removing the veil in the spirit and allowing you to see the spiritual battle going on.

The Scriptures indicate that there are three "heavens." The first is the natural, Adamic realm where time, space, and matter exist. The second heaven is the spiritual dimension surrounding the earth and is where demonic activities can occur, along with angelic activities.

> *I know a man in Christ who fourteen years ago— whether in the body I do not know, or whether out of the body I do not know, God knows—such a one was caught up to the third heaven* (2 Corinthians 12:2).

> *For we do not wrestle against flesh and blood, but against principalities, against powers, against the rulers of the darkness of this age, against spiritual hosts of wickedness in the heavenly places* (Ephesians 6:12).

The third heaven is where God's home resides. I also believe that there are multiple levels both in the heavenlies and in hell.

As a young Christian, I needed to grow into the prophetic. I needed to exercise and practice discernment as Hebrews teaches:

*For everyone who partakes only of milk is unskilled
in the word of righteousness, for he is a babe. But
solid food belongs to those who are of full age, that is,
those who by reason of use have their senses exercised
to discern both good and evil* (Hebrews 5:13-14).

I have discovered that one of the biggest errors prophetic Christians can fall into is misinterpreting what they are seeing in the heavenlies. When Christians operate out of the second heaven they can become quite depressed, and this is very dangerous because we are called to live out of the third heaven and have dominion over the second and first heavens. This happened to me, and I used to walk around looking miserable. People used to comment on how miserable I looked, and one person said to me years ago, "Why would I want to become a Christian like you? You look miserable!"

I used to see so much demonic activity, and it used to depress me. I thought these events were the foregone conclusion of the world's end. I fell into the trap of becoming an extreme alarmist—there was nothing but doom and gloom, and I believed the world was coming to an end because of these visions I was experiencing. I wasn't aware at the time that God was removing the veil for me to see what was going on in the heavenlies. He was allowing me to witness the plans of the enemy ahead of time. This was the grace of God to show me the plans of the enemy and then give me the strategies to bind and shut down these demonic powers and activities by the power of the blood of

Jesus Christ. God gave me the authority to take dominion over the heavenlies, which then started to change the atmosphere in the natural realm—the first heaven.

> *I have discovered that one of the biggest errors prophetic Christians can fall into is misinterpreting what they are seeing in the heavenlies.*

One of the times I was ministering in India, God gave me a vivid vision of me being viciously attacked by a bull. Cows are seen as holy and are worshiped in India, and the Lord said to me that this bull is a principality in the heavenlies that was opposed to me being there. God gave me this warning, so I got into the spirit and bound this principality with the blood of Jesus and commanded it to be shut down. This led to one of our most successful trips where we witnessed many dedications to Christ, healings, and miracles. God's glory broke out in this area. On the east coast, the Hindu extremists came up against the church I was due to minister at. They set fire to the church and put a knife to the throat of the pastor, threatening him of death if he allowed me to speak. Each time, though, God gave me a warning and showed me how to deal with the principalities and powers of darkness. His grace and privileges overflowed, not only into my life but the lives of others, and it can flow into your life as well.

Another way God communicates with us is through words of knowledge in dreams and visions—this is receiving names or knowing the sicknesses or circumstances in a person's life. As I worship and soak before a meeting, God will show me what He wants to do in that meeting through words of knowledge. This can also be very helpful when you are counseling someone or interpreting a nightmare. Words of knowledge can guide you in understanding why a person is experiencing nightmares. In some instances, a person can open themselves up to the demonic realm, giving the enemy permission in their lives by speaking death into a situation, by lacking faith, or by indulging in things they should not. All of these can open a doorway to the enemy and allow him to come in and destroy your life.

As I worship and soak before a meeting, God will show me what He wants to do in that meeting through words of knowledge.

Words of knowledge help you to pinpoint the areas that need to be focused on. I was in Borneo with Todd Weatherly and Neil Porch—Neil speaks fluent Indonesian and he is our interpreter when we travel in Indonesia. On this particular day, we were going from home to home to pray for the sick. We had a house visit with a lady who attended church, but her home had such a heavy oppression over it and her daughter was brain damaged and hadn't been able to walk for years. This damage happened when she had a high temperature and without medical treatment the temperature actually got high enough to begin to cook her brain. As we were ministering to this family, I received a word of knowledge through a vision revealing that the mother was operating in witchcraft. She denied it at first but eventually confessed. She repented of it and rededicated her life to Christ, and as she did we felt a shift in the atmosphere. God showed us the demonic power operating in the daughter's life, and we began to pray against it. In faith I told her that she needed to get up and walk. Within three days she was completely healed. I prophesied over her life that God was going to use her mightily for the nation of Indonesia. You can view the three days of progressive healing on YouTube.

We can operate in this heavenly realm. This is how Jesus operated, and it is our birthright to do the things that the Father does and say the things that the Father says.

chapter 7

THE SANCTIFIED IMAGINATION

As I mentioned before, we are made up of three elements—the mind, body, and spirit. The mind is attached to the
soul, the spirit man is the subconscious, and the physical body
contains the brain. In this chapter I want to focus on the mind.
The Holy Spirit can communicate with us through our subconscious mind or our spirit man. We can't fabricate dreams
through our mind; the Holy Spirit speaks to us through His
sovereignty operating through the subconscious mind. Our
spirit man can be exposed to the heavenlies, but our mind has
been fashioned in order to create. Our mind is part of our will,
and our will determines what we want to do, such as what
we want to eat or wear. We can meditate and create thoughts
through the use of our minds.

The enemy has no authority over us (see 1 John 4:4). We have the authority to trample on snakes and scorpions and overcome all the powers of darkness (see Luke 10:19). So we are untouchable in Christ as a part of His family. However, the enemy can attack, harass, and torment us through the mind. The enemy cannot physically touch us, but he can con us. He is like a bad used-car salesman who uses deception to con people. God created the mind to create, but the mind can exaggerate and distort things as well, and the enemy knows our minds and how to use them.

The enemy knows that fear is his greatest weapon, and he wants to torment us through the use of fear by playing it out in our minds. Our minds are used for creating, but they can also work in a negative way by thriving on fear. If our mind meditates on ungodly thoughts or fear, the enemy has an open door to deceive us into making wrong decisions. He uses fear to cause us to react in ways we should not. The enemy starts using fear on us from a young age—children are exposed to television programs that often have demonic themes. He wants to start with the very young and expose them to fear and anxiety, opening ungodly doors. The enemy is operating through these shows. Take Walt Disney movies—at first they look very innocent, very colorful and friendly, but underneath is often fear or demonic themes.

Recently, I went to the movies with my son and we saw an advertisement for *Snow White and the Huntsman*. It was so demonic, and the special effects created an atmosphere of fear to torment people. This is a children's fantasy story, the movie is quite demonic and terrifying. The enemy uses fear in the movies to influence children. I find movies like *Harry Potter* to be quite evil. I have not watched all of them but I have seen some snippets, and my thoughts and convictions are that if you are a Christian and you enjoy these movies something is very wrong in your relationship with God. The themes of this series are quite demonic—they incorporate witchcraft, fear, and magic. People of the world are obsessed with *Harry Potter*; the books are some of the best sellers in history, and that is because people thrive on fear. Fear is the reverse of faith. A whole generation is indulging in fear, and this opens a doorway to the demonic realm, inviting demonic powers to torment us.

> *The enemy cannot physically touch us, but he can con us. He is like a bad used-car salesman who uses deception to con people.*

There is another unholy revival that has broken out through the youth of this time—they are obsessed with movies like *Twilight* and television shows like *The Vampire Diaries*. Obsession with vampires, werewolves, blood, and fear indulges in the demonic realm. A whole generation has come into the realm of fear, and some teenagers actually believe that they are real vampires. They have parties where they sharpen their teeth and partake in vampire-like activities, biting and sucking the blood of one another. My conviction is that if you believe in something enough you become it. You become consumed by demonic powers in the heavenlies, and as you begin to channel them you become controlled by them.

Hollywood actors can operate in this realm without even realizing it. There are some amazing actors out there who are very talented, but unfortunately the way to their success is through channeling the aspects of the character written in the script. They meditate and become absorbed with their script character to eventually take on that character. This was clearly demonstrated through the tragic death of Australian-born actor Heath Ledger. My thoughts and prayers are with his family, and I have compassion over this situation and how it has affected them. Heath Ledger took on and channeled the character of the Joker in his last movie, *The Dark Knight.* I believe that through his obsession and constant meditation on the Joker's character, Heath opened the wrong door to the spirit realm. *"For as he thinks in his heart, so is he"* (Prov. 23:7). Jack Nicholson warned Heath Ledger about taking on this Joker character, as it was consuming him. There was an article in the *New York Daily News* headlined: "Jack Nicholson Warned Heath Ledger on Joker Role." The article stated:

> Ledger recently told reporters he "slept an average of two hours a night" while playing "a psychopathic, mass-murdering, schizophrenic clown with zero empathy...I couldn't stop thinking. My body

was exhausted, and my mind was still going." Prescription drugs didn't help, he said.[1]

> *My conviction is that if you believe in something enough you become it.*

On set, Michael Caine said the performance sometimes turned so frightening he forgot his own lines. This opened a door to darkness and may have contributed to Heath's death.

The same doorway to the demonic realm can be opened by other religions. For example, Buddhist monks take on demons calling it reincarnation—that is their interpretation of the process. They visualize and meditate on spirits for years and take on the demonic powers from the second heavens. Some monks take on these demons and become totally possessed by them; others unfortunately don't make it that far and actually become insane or die. The documentary *Furious Love* by Darren Wilson showed what happened to some Tibetan monks who had used visualization to take on these spirits and how it negatively affected them and actually drove them mad.

I have to explain all this before I can go into something godly, for the same method of using your mind can apply to godly ways. The above is a counterfeit of the real thing. We, in a holy and sanctified way, can meditate using the mind. The New International Version uses the word *imagine*:

*Now to him who is able to do immeasurably more than all we ask or **imagine**, according to his power that is at work within us* (Ephesians 3:20 NIV, emphasis added).

> *We, in a holy and sanctified way, can meditate using the mind.*

Imagining is making use of the mind. We need to focus our eyes on Jesus, who is the author and finisher of our faith (Heb. 12:2). This refers to our spiritual eyes, which use our imagination. God requires us to meditate on Him. Colossians says that we are to focus on the things above, as we are seated in heavenly places:

If then you were raised with Christ, seek those things which are above, where Christ is, sitting at the right hand of God. Set your mind on things above, not on things on the earth (Colossians 3:1-2).

But put on the Lord Jesus Christ, and make no provision for the flesh, to fulfill its lusts (Romans 13:14).

And Jesus said:

But I say to you that whoever looks at a woman to lust for her has already committed adultery with her in his heart (Matthew 5:28).

This shows that something is activated in the spirit. When a man is using his imagination, he is using his spiritual eyes. In using his imagination in this way, a door can be opened to the spirit realm. If he is using it in an unholy way it opens up to the second heaven, which in this case attracts the spirit of lust. Matthew 5 further states:

> *If your right eye causes you to sin, pluck it out and cast it from you; for it is more profitable for you that one of your members perish, than for your whole body to be cast into hell* (Matthew 5:29).

I believe there is a layer of revelation to this. The right eye is a metaphor for your spiritual eye or imagination, and I believe that what Jesus is saying is that if your imagination causes you to sin, you need to shut it down.

What we do not see is more real than what we do see, and therefore we need to ensure that we are focusing on godly things. There are people who meditate on unholy things, and this is prevalent in Internet usage. The Internet has the best and worst of information; it is like a modern-day tree of knowledge of good and evil. People are fixing their eyes on pornography, violence, and horror themes, meditating on them; this activates the imagination and opens the door to the demonic realm. Jesus said that if your eye is bad your whole body is bad (see Matt 6:23). If you are opening a door through the gateway of your spiritual eyes to unholy things, you start storing up negative images in your imagination, and they become the focus of your meditation. This allows Satan to have access to your mind.

> *What we do not see is more real*
> *than what we do see.*

Satan wants his will done on earth as it is in hell. How often have you heard people ask, "What is the world coming to?" There are horrible news reports daily, and I believe this is because people are meditating on ungodly things. They are opening up portals to the demonic realm, and we are witnessing a spillover of hell manifesting on earth.

However, you can reverse this thought pattern in a holy and sanctified manner and use the imagination to build an intimate relationship with the Lord. The Lord Jesus Christ, in a holy way, is our eternal lover, mother, father, and brother all in one. In a sanctified manner, we can use our spiritual eyes to worship the Lord in spirit and in truth, and we will witness the activation of the spirit realm. Meditate on His promises based on the foundation of the Word. If we use our imaginations to pursue the things of God, heavenly doors will open, once this activation in the spirit occurs. When you start to use your imagination during worship, you are actually opening a door to the Lord. This is the essence of our Christian walk—worship.

Behold, I stand at the door and knock. If anyone
hears My voice and opens the door, I will come in to

him and dine with him, and he with Me (Revelation 3:20).

Lift up your heads, O you gates! And be lifted up, you everlasting doors! And the King of glory shall come in (Psalm 24:7).

In studying this Scripture, I found that one translation stated that when you lift up your head it is a form of worship. Jesus said that when you see troubles in the world you are to lift up your head and know that the time is near (see Luke 21:28). This lifting up of the head can mean worship. We are the gates that are to usher in the Kingdom of Heaven here on earth. I believe the ancient doors are the entry into the eternal realm, and as we lift up our heads as the gates we tap into the eternal realm. Through this worship the King of Glory will come in. Once we do this, we become intimate with our Lord and will start to experience encounters with Him. These can be supernatural encounters, like receiving visions and healings. Revelation of the Kingdom of Heaven can be unveiled through the revelatory realm.

I would like to share a testimony of when I received a healing through worshiping God. It wasn't a major healing, but it was still powerful in that it changed my life. One winter I was lying on the couch worshiping God. My family had gone to bed, and after a while I fell asleep. I woke up needing to go to the bathroom, but I couldn't bring myself to put my feet down and stand up to get off the couch because we had a slate floor which was freezing cold and I had no slippers to put on my feet. More importantly, I was fearful because, when I was a child, my mother used to say that I had to put shoes on when it was cold—I couldn't run around in bare feet or I would get a runny nose. My grandfather also said I would catch a cold if I had no shoes on and walked on a cold floor.

> *We are the gates that are to usher in the Kingdom of Heaven here on earth.*

God bless them, for at the time they did not realize that by saying this they actually spoke a curse over me and a soul tie was created. As an adult, every time I walked barefoot over a cold floor I would instantly start to get a runny nose, and sometimes the runny nose lasted for days. This verbal curse through my soul ties to my mother and grandfather allowed the enemy to attack me and take away my health.

I was lying there hearing the echo of my mother's voice: "You're going to get a runny nose!" I went back to worshiping the Lord. I wanted to be back in His presence, and I asked Him what I should do. The Lord said to me that I should start meditating on His Word by using my imagination. John 15 says, *"If you abide in Me, and My words abide in you, you will ask what you desire, and it shall be done for you"* (John 15:7). So on this promise, I started to use my imagination and built up the idea that the slate floor had central heating. I believed it so much that I could eventually get up and walk to the bathroom. In time, I went back to the couch, and I did not have a runny nose! Nothing happened! You might be thinking, *Big deal, Adam!* To me it was a big deal—I had *always* had a runny nose after walking barefoot on cold floors. God delivered me from this fear through the use of my imagination.

After this experience, I fell asleep and I was caught up in a vision and had an encounter with the Lord in the third heaven. I was walking on a massive sea of glass. It reminded me of when John got caught up into the third heaven: *"Before the throne there was a sea of glass, like crystal"* (Rev. 4:6). I didn't see a throne in my encounter, but I was walking on this sea of glass, and I felt such life spring up in my lungs. I felt truly alive! I remember thinking what an incredible place this was as my lungs were filled with life. After a while, I realized that this sea of glass felt as if it had central heating in it. I felt so comfortable and at peace, and I marveled at the feelings I was experiencing, both emotionally and physically as my feet were warm. The Spirit of God said to me, "Whatever you ask for already exists in Heaven. It is the testimony of Jesus that whatever you ask for is already here." This is within reason of course—a sanctified request and the desires God has put within you already exist in Heaven. I came out of this encounter and it changed my life.

A week later, I was spending time worshiping the Lord and I fell asleep. Again, I was caught up into an encounter on the sea of glass in the third heaven. This time it seemed as if I was closer to the throne of God, which looked like a dome of gold light. The closer I got, the brighter and bigger this gold light became. I didn't see the throne because of the intensity of the bright and glorious light, but I knew the throne was in there.

> *"Whatever you ask for already exists in Heaven. It is the testimony of Jesus that whatever you ask for is already here."*

I saw thousands and thousands of empty crystal chairs embedded into the sea of glass. I wondered why these chairs were empty; I thought some event must have occurred in the past or one was about to take place, because I was the only one there. The Spirit of God spoke to me again and said that these were the seats of the saints who have been robbed of the revelatory understanding of what it means to be seated in heavenly places. The Lord showed me that a lot of Christians are walking their spiritual life using their country of earthly citizenship to serve God. They don't understand their identity in God or what it means to be seated in heavenly places. They are walking in authority, but not in a posture. Their minds are constantly being tormented by fear, and they are not secure in God—they are walking in unbelief.

I had another encounter with the Lord just recently. In a supernatural dream, I was preaching in front of a multitude—I believe in Australia—and I said, "You come to me and say you can't hear the voice of God; you come to me because you want a word. The Lord will say to you, *'You come to Me saying I can't hear the voice of God; I'm having trouble hearing God; but you have no trouble in listening to the lies of the Devil.'* Listening to him creates fear, anxiety, frustration, and doubt. The Lord says use your ears to hear His promises and walk in them with your spiritual eyes and the anointed imagination."

> *'You come to Me saying I can't hear*
> *the voice of God; I'm having trouble*
> *hearing God; but you have no trouble*
> *in listening to the lies of the Devil.'*

This is the true meaning of what it is to be set apart. The religious mentality says you must be set apart physically, as if you should live in a cave. The sanctified meaning of being set apart is changing your thinking. Instead of having your mind attached to the soulish part of your being, discipline it to be attached to the things and the promises of God. Live out of that realm where you are meditating constantly on the purposes of God—then you will start to recognize the sovereign voice of the Lord speaking to you. If we all operate like this corporately, then we will see revival hit earth and witness a community change. That is the time when you will walk the way Jesus walked.

You will walk in complete peace, and you will have authority with a sound mind. Second Timothy says, *"For God has not given us a spirit of fear, but of power and of love and of a sound mind"* (2 Tim. 1:7). You become completely at peace, and you won't be walking in a realm of fear and torment. *"You will keep him in perfect peace, whose mind is stayed on You, because he trusts in You"* (Isa. 26:3). When we trust in God, we will keep in perfect peace.

> *Finally, brethren, whatever things are true, whatever things are noble, whatever things are just, whatever things are pure, whatever things are lovely, whatever things are of good report, if there is any virtue and if there is anything praiseworthy—meditate on these things. The things which you learned and received and heard and saw in me, these do, and the God of peace will be with you* (Philippians 4:8-9).

When we trust in God, we will keep in perfect peace.

Our mind is very powerful, and I believe our sanctified imagination plays a big part in walking in the supernatural.

ENDNOTE

1. Joe Neumaier, "Jack Nicholson Warned Heath Ledger on Joker Role," NY Daily News, January 24, 2008, accessed February 03, 2013, http://www.nydailynews.com/news/jack-nicholson -warned-heath-ledger-joker-role-article-1.340786.

chapter 8

WALKING IN THE
SUPERNATURAL

IN THIS BOOK, I HAVE MENTIONED A LOT OF TESTIMONIES, experiences, and encounters that I have had. Walking in the supernatural, visitations to Heaven, seeing angels, and having visions is a part of my life. It is something to encounter the Lord and have these experiences, but it is another thing to be a carrier of God's glory and bring the experiential reality into the wider community.

In Matthew we read:

> *Now after six days Jesus took Peter, James, and John his brother, led them up on a high mountain by themselves; and He was transfigured before them. His face shone like the sun, and His clothes*

> *became as white as the light. And behold, Moses*
> *and Elijah appeared to them, talking with Him*
> (Matthew 17:1-3).

The glory of God came down, and the disciples had an amazing encounter with Jesus, Elijah, and Moses. I believe this was an encounter where the disciples saw Jesus's true form. They were in the eternal realm; it was another time zone, and this is the revelation given to me—this was showing who Jesus truly is. He is the *I AM*, the Alpha and Omega, the First and the Last, the Beginning and the End. I believe that when the disciples saw Elijah and Moses standing with Jesus, time stood still. All of the time zones and times in history across the earth came together at this one moment. There was no time, space, or matter at this one moment in the eternal realm, and this was more real than what we see. Peter was in awe of the glory of God and wanted to set up three tabernacles; I believe that he did not want to come out of this experience, even though some commentaries basically say that Peter did not know what he was talking about. As they came down from the mountain, Jesus said to His disciples not to tell anyone of this vision. The chapter continues:

> *And when they had come to the multitude, a man*
> *came to Him, kneeling down to Him and saying,*
> *"Lord, have mercy on my son, for he is an epilep-*
> *tic and suffers severely; for he often falls into the*
> *fire and often into the water. So I brought him to*
> *Your disciples, but they could not cure him." Then*

Jesus answered and said, "O faithless and perverse generation, how long shall I be with you? How long shall I bear with you? Bring him here to Me." And Jesus rebuked the demon, and it came out of him; and the child was cured from that very hour. Then the disciples came to Jesus privately and said, "Why could we not cast it out?" (Matthew 17:14-19)

I believe that Peter, James, and John experienced an anti-climax after the experience on the mountain. They weren't in faith—they did not know how to bring the glory down from the mountain top and be carriers of it. Jesus—God with skin on—was a forerunner for us as a carrier of the glory. Through the finished work of the cross and the revelation of what Jesus accomplished, we inherit everything Jesus has. We therefore have the ability to become carriers. This is the beauty of being a Christian—we have everything that Jesus has.

To the disciples, the transfiguration on the mountain was just an experience rather than a way of life, which is why they suffered an anti-climax. They didn't realize that they were still with the same Jesus—the one who is the same yesterday, today, and forever. We need to know the reality of Jesus in us—the Alpha and the Omega, the one transfigured on the mountain top.

In my Christian walk, I've grown into the prophetic and the supernatural. I came out of being a workaholic businessman and moved into the realm of living in the supernatural. Back in the early days, about ten years ago, I was working out my spiritual walk and my prophetic gifting. I would have encounters, but when I came out of them I had no idea what to do with them—I felt useless. I even had pastors say, "Well, yeah, that Adam, he's more vertical than horizontal." They were implying that I was useless in the natural. I would have these amazing experiences of being on the mountain top with God, and then all of a sudden I would be back in the natural and my wife would be handing me the rubbish to take out and I was useless in even doing that.

> *To the disciples, the transfiguration on the mountain was just an experience rather than a way of life, which is why they suffered an anti-climax.*

My conviction is that there is a time for everything; Ecclesiastes 3 describes how everything has its time. There is a time to wait upon the Lord and there is a time to act. In the book of Acts, the apostles acted upon God's Word:

> *And being assembled together with them, He commanded them not to depart from Jerusalem, but to wait for the Promise of the Father, "which," He said, "you have heard from Me"* (Acts 1:4).

They had to wait to receive power. In Acts 2, God poured out His Spirit, and they encountered the supernatural on the day of Pentecost; metaphorically, they had a mountain-top experience. Peter delivered one of his best sermons after this infilling of the Holy Spirit, and he quoted the words spoken by the prophet Joel. The disciples *acted* upon this experience—they stepped out and supernatural signs and wonders were released into the community, which changed the world. Some of the disciples stayed in Jerusalem—they wanted to remain in that experience. Acts 8 shows how persecution came upon the church in Jerusalem as some of the disciples remained and would not step out. This persecution scattered them and forced them to preach the gospel. Philip got an Ethiopian saved through supernatural means.

I believe that for us in the modern-day church it is very good to have mountain-top experiences and receive revelation in God's presence. If we don't bring His presence into the community and don't become carriers of God's glory—walking as Jesus walked and bringing the experiential manifestation of the glory and releasing it through signs and wonders—then I believe that persecution will come.

There are so many counterfeit religions out there that are trying to have a great influence on our community; this is an anti-Christ spirit trying to penetrate society. Some of these religions are quite wealthy and have a lot of influence, but we as Christians need to make a stand for the Kingdom of God. We either step out now by faith or we will be forced to do it through persecution. I'm not saying bringing the Kingdom of God to the community is only by doing good and helping the poor. Jesus said that you will always have the poor, and unbelievers and unbelieving organizations help the poor as well.

> *If we don't bring His presence into the community and don't become carriers of God's glory—walking as Jesus walked and bringing the experiential manifestation of the glory and releasing it through signs and wonders— then I believe that persecution will come.*

How God anointed Jesus of Nazareth with the Holy Spirit and power, and how he went around doing good and healing all who were under the power of the devil, because God was with him (Acts 10:38 NIV).

We need to bring the supernatural into the community with signs and wonders. Helping the poor is a given; one of the essences of God's nature is love, and we need to reflect His love. The supernatural attribute of Jesus and our gifting can open the door for people to receive the truth. *"A man's gift makes room for him, and brings him before great men"* (Prov. 18:16). On many levels this is talking about your gift, and I believe this applies to the gifts of the Spirit with supernatural manifestations of signs and wonders. They pave the way and can give you a platform to preach the Word—to tell people the gospel of Jesus Christ.

Miracles will always get people's attention. Here is one account of some amazing miracles and their impact on the community.

Tommy Hicks was a catalyst for the Argentinean revival; before this he was not a well-known man. Wanting to go deeper with God, Tommy went on a 40-day fast, and after it ended nothing happened. So again he went on another 40-day fast, and again nothing happened. He went on a third 40-day fast. After the third 40-day fast, he was met by an angel of the Lord. The angel said that God wanted him to sell everything he had and go to Argentina. His wife had a vision and saw a sickle in his hand sifting through a wheat field shaped as a map of Argentina. Tommy obeyed the calling of God and flew to Argentina. While he was sitting on the airplane, Tommy heard the audible voice of God telling him to speak to a man named Mr. Peron.

> *They pave the way and can give you a platform to preach the Word—to tell people the gospel of Jesus Christ. Miracles will always get people's attention.*

Tommy had no idea who this Mr. Peron was, so he asked the air hostess if there was a man named "Peron" in her country. She replied that that was the name of the President, Juan Peron. When he arrived in Argentina, Tommy went to the parliament gates and requested the guard let him see the President. The armed guard laughed at Tommy—everyone wanted to see President Peron, even his own mother wanted to. Tommy began telling the guard about the healing crusade God told him to host. The guard was captivated about this talk of God and asked if God could heal him—he was in a lot of pain as a result of having Hepatitis C. Tommy told him to take his hand and he prayed for him, and instantly the guard was completely healed. The guard told Tommy, "Come back tomorrow and I'll get you in to see the President."

This was a great miracle in itself—the guard was miraculously healed and now Tommy would have an audience with the President. Peron heard about the miracle healing of the guard, and he asked Tommy how he could be of help. Tommy said he was there on a mandate from God to do a salvation and healing campaign and requested the use of a large stadium and press and radio coverage. Peron asked if Tommy's Jesus could heal him—he had been suffering from a permanent and disfiguring skin condition known as psoriasis. Tommy clasped hands with Peron, and as he prayed the power of God was released into Peron and he was instantly and completely healed.

Peron said Tommy could have whatever he wanted. He called in the media and advertising agencies. One article states:

> The Atlantic Stadium [Estadio Don León Kolbovski] with a seating capacity of 25,000 was rented. Soon overwhelming crowds forced them to relocate to the Huracán Football Stadium [Estadio Tomás Adolfo Ducó] with a seating capacity

of 110,000, which also overflowed. In two months 3 million were reported to have attended with 300,000 decisions for Christ and a massive number of outstanding healings.[1]

> *Tommy clasped hands with Peron, and as he prayed the power of God was released into Peron and he was instantly and completely healed.*

The healings in these crusades were so amazing and powerful that they had to have semi trucks come into the stadiums to pick up the crutches and wheelchairs that were abandoned after the meetings.

Another great revivalist was Evan Roberts. After a powerful infilling of the Holy Spirit at a meeting, Evan began to pray for the salvation of a hundred thousand souls. He received two visions from God confirming that this would happen. In the first vision:

> He saw a lighted candle and behind it the rising sun. He felt the interpretation was that the present blessings were only as a lighted candle compared with the blazing glory of the sun. Later all Wales would be flooded with revival glory. The other vision occurred when Evan saw his close friend Sydney Evans staring at the moon. Evan asked what he was looking at and, to his great surprise,

he saw it too! It was an arm that seemed to be out-stretched from the moon down to Wales. He was in no doubt that revival was on its way.[2]

This revival, known as the Welsh Revival, changed a nation and was one of the biggest revivals on record. This revival was so big it eventually spread worldwide. Police stations had to lay off policemen as they were no longer needed, pubs shut down as no one was buying alcohol, and brothels turned into home fellowships as the prostitutes repented and became born again and spent their days praising and working for the Lord. The soccer grand finals used to be on every year, but this particular year was the first time in history that no grand final occurred due to the revival. This revival came from visions, and it affected the community, spread out to the nation, and eventually to other nations.

You, too, can be a carrier of God's glory and affect your community. I want to coach you on how to step out from what you see and bring down that experience from the mountain top. What you receive during visions or encounters with Heaven—what God shows you that He wants you to do—needs to be released to the community and brought into reality as an experiential manifestation.

In Chapter 7, I explained a bit of how I position myself with the Lord. I worship Him, I engage my imagination, and I soak in His presence. Then I go into a place where I wait upon Him; in this trance-like sleep, the Lord downloads what He wants me to do, either in the church meeting or in my daily life. This is a fast-track teaching for you. I had to grow in this, and I had to learn from my mistakes. I received so many visions in my growing years that I did not know what to do with them. Many prophets receive visions but don't know what to do with them; they have not received discernment on what the Spirit of the Lord is saying to them—whether it is something God wants them to step out on or whether it is a metaphor. As you practice it you will become sharper, and you will grow into that prophetic calling.

Police stations had to lay off policemen as they were no longer needed, pubs shut down as no one was buying alcohol, and brothels turned into home fellowships as the prostitutes repented and became born again and spent their days praising and working for the Lord.

There was a time when I was soaking and I received a vision of a man with a really damaged eyed. He lost his eye and he had a glass eye in its place; there were even fake eyelashes attached to the eyelid. The look of this eye really disturbed me and I wondered why I had seen it. Two hours later, after I came out of the vision, I had to go to a tire shop to get my punctured tire fixed. As I walked into the shop I saw the tire fitter had the exact same artificial eye with fake eyelashes. The surgeon obviously had tried to fix the eye as best he could, but it was still very disturbing and I had no idea what to do. I remember going back to my car and driving off, and I asked God why had I seen that exact same disturbing eye as in the vision. God said, "Adam, come on, wake up! I showed you that so you could pray for the man. I was showing you who you were going to meet today." God told me a day later that if I had prayed for that man He would have healed him. I felt inadequate, as I had missed the opportunity to pray for someone to be healed.

What I am about to say may be controversial, but it is real. The Lord has shown me that many of us read the Bible and hear the information and retain it. This is the *logos* word which gets stored up inside. I, too, have this *logos* word sown inside me—the word is just like seeds. I can quote Scriptures on the spot and I have many memorized, and I can also tell you what a lot of chapters in the Bible contain. This is all very good, but it's just seeds sitting inside of me. Lots of Christians have this information, but God wants the seeds to be illuminated and to become revelation. Once the word becomes revelation—the *rhema* word—it becomes substance for a person to step out in confidence. Revelation is like the light turning on; when you finally get the meaning behind the word it becomes real to you. I believe this is the part where your imagination comes into play.

This is how I do things, just as Jesus taught me; I believe it is very powerful, and this is how I operate. I have witnessed many miracles from this process. I've mentioned how I soak and wait upon the Lord. When I get downloads from God, I snap out of the vision and I immediately write the images, visions, and words down. God will show me what He wants me to do in church meetings or in my daily life. Then I go back to soaking and I start exercising my imagination.

> *Revelation is like the light turning on;*
> *when you finally get the meaning behind*
> *the word it becomes real to you.*

For example, let's say I see a woman with a particular hair color who is limping in a vision. I will come out of the vision and write it down, and then I will go back into a place of soaking and start to build up my imagination around that image. I will imagine myself stepping out, laying hands on the woman, and praying for her. I will see her foot growing and aligning with the other foot in my mind. I will build up this image in my imagination until it becomes real to me. Our spiritual eyes and imagination play a big part when it comes to the miraculous.

I believe there is a fine line between imagination and visualization. Visualization can mean recalling a past experience stored up in your mind and stirring it up, sort of like meditating on testimonies. Jesus said to His disciples at the Last Supper when He broke the bread, *"...do this in remembrance of Me"* (Luke 22:19). He was saying this to encourage us to bring a *past* testimony into a *now* reality of the power of the cross. Imagination is quite creative, and its focus is on new experiences of what you are going to do in the future.

In order for us to move in the supernatural, the images of the testimony of the past which are placed in our minds need to manifest; then we can start building upon them as God starts to speak of miracles. God shows us what He wants us to do through spontaneous visions which we receive from the Holy Spirit through our subconscious mind. To build your faith and be encouraged in the Lord, it is helpful to meditate on past experiences, miracles, and testimonies in order to successfully create new ones for the future. The testimony of Jesus is the spirit of prophecy, so I believe God wants us to recall these past testimonies and recreate them based on the promises of God. If you want to see great miracles, you need to create new images in your mind and create them on the foundation of His Word. For example, in Isaiah it says, *"...by His stripes we are healed"* (Isa. 53:5). This is the foundation, but we have to create the images in our minds in order to break into new experiences and miracles.

Our imaginations are extremely powerful, and unfortunately as young children we are sometimes discouraged from using our imaginations. Some people in the natural will debunk the use of the imagination, stating that they are realists and that the use of the imagination will lead to disappointment. I believe that the people who succeed in this world, whether they are Christians or not, usually have used their imaginations to dream big dreams, and then they have acted upon them. The more you imagine operating in miracles, signs, and wonders, the more you start to believe it and step out to perform it.

"Now faith is the substance of things hoped for, the evidence of things not seen" (Heb. 11:1). Based on this verse, I believe your imagination comes from hope, and the more it is used the more your faith is increased. That gives you the power to act upon it and decree it. Be careful when you speak it out, though, as it can be just human positive thinking if there is no real belief behind it. You need faith in situations and that "you know that you know" feeling when decreeing what your imagination has created. On the *rhema* word, faith is the substance and substance is the reality.

> *The people who succeed in this world, whether they are Christians or not, usually have used their imaginations to dream big dreams, and then they have acted upon them.*

My imagination has become very powerful, and I have learned to develop and exercise it over the years. Once I was in Hong Kong ministering, and as I was waiting upon the Lord before a meeting with a bottle of water in my hand, I had a vision of a gold vessel that had oil from Heaven in it. I started acting upon this vision by using my imagination. At first I could see the vessel in my mind, and then I became able to "see" myself pouring the oil out. I kept replaying this image and it became stronger in my mind, but what I did not realize was that physically I had started to put actions to the image in my mind and I had poured out the water from my bottle. There was water everywhere!

As you become more in-depth in experiencing the supernatural realm, you may find at times the natural and supernatural realms can overlap. You need to be alert to distinguish the differences between the two. This can be dangerous if you are using it outside the counsel of God in an unholy way to satisfy your soulish desires.

> *Son of man, prophesy against the prophets of Israel who prophesy, and say to those who prophesy out of their own heart, "Hear the word of the Lord!"* (Ezekiel 13:2)

This verse clearly shows that the prophets were prophesying out of their imaginations from soulish desires. These prophets didn't build anything; they were like foxes in the desert and watchmen who did not protect. They were not in tune with the Spirit of God, and they were not listening to God's word. They were just prophesying to have their own agendas accomplished. They were prophesying outside the counsel of God's word, which is known as divination.

We need to be careful of not getting caught up in operating our imaginations from the soulish part of us. There is a big responsibility to using our imaginations; they need to be used with faith for building up the glory of God and not for our own agendas or negativity. That would be operating out of manipulation and fear, which only opens the door to darkness.

Sometimes my imagination is so real to me that I can actually taste and smell it. Once I imagined gas! I was building my imagination on an experience at a gas station where I had led someone to Christ. As I was building up my imagination, I could actually smell the gas. A friend of mine, Kathy Walters, moves in a realm in the spirit where she can smell different fragrances. Her mind and spirit man are really open to the Spirit of God, and she is able to see, smell, and taste things both in the spirit and in the natural.

We need to be careful of not getting caught up in operating our imaginations from the soulish part of us.

Here is a quick example. Let's say you go to a restaurant, and this particular restaurant does not have any images on its menu—everything is in text form. When you look at the contents of dishes, you try to imagine what the dish is going to look like. You try to create an image of how the dish is going to be presented to you in your imagination based on the words written, as there are no images to guide your choice. When the actual meal comes out you can be disappointed, because it does not look like the image you had in your mind. The other dinner guests' meals look so much better than yours. Asian restaurants are famous for their big images, both on the menus and at the counter boards. When you see the images and how good the food looks it starts to whet your appetite, and you begin to imagine how good the food is going to taste. This gives you the confidence to order the dish that most appeals to you, and often you are not disappointed when the food comes out because you were already expecting it to taste good.

Here's another example. Let's say I gave several people a tomato seed, each without telling them what kind of seed it is. If I asked what kind of seed they thought it was, most people would not have the confidence to say what fruit the seed would produce. Only a few would guess that it was a tomato seed. Some may know for sure, but some of these people wouldn't have the confidence to step out and plant this seed if they don't know what they are going to get. But if you got the seed out of the packet it was packaged in, the image of the big red juicy tomato would immediately show you what kind of seed was inside. There is a vision attached to the seed. The vision gives you the confidence and the faith to act upon it and plant that seed.

Another translation of the word *vision* is revelation. The apostle John wrote the book of Revelation, which is a book containing visions. When you see the vision attached to the seed, you are given the confidence and faith to step out. In this example, the seed is the Word of God. Your imagination starts building around that seed, and this gives you the confidence to step out, act upon it, and start decreeing it. Great sportsmen use their imagination to build upon their physical movements. For example, tennis players will imagine every swing needed to hit the ball, and they will imagine an entire game and its outcome before they physically play a game.

My brother-in-law is a pilot, and recently he had to change airlines. He had to practice using a simulator for all of his new flight paths and countries. He had to use the simulator over and over again to build his confidence to such a point where he could anticipate the flight routes and handle any incidents without any second-guessing. It became second nature to him, and this has helped him in his job. He used the images given to him and practiced them both in his mind and physically, which has made him great at his job.

> *Your imagination starts building around that seed, and this gives you the confidence to step out, act upon it, and start decreeing it.*

Here's an example and a few testimonies of when I had to move out in faith. I was at Field of Dreams church in South Australia a few years ago. Before the meeting, while soaking in God's presence, I went into a trance and had a vision of a woman. This woman was getting a blood test and I knew she had a problem with her blood. I started to pray for this woman, and using my imagination I saw the blood in her body being completely restored. I had no idea what the problem was; my focus was on the outcome and not the problem. Based on the Word of God that by His stripes we are healed, I saw her healed.

A couple of hours later, I was in the meeting and I called it out as a word of knowledge, "There is a woman here who has had some blood tests to check certain levels. You are very concerned about the result, but I want to tell you that the Lord has healed you!" A woman came up and responded to the word of knowledge. She had Hepatitis C, and in the natural this cannot be cured, but I prayed for her, stepped out in faith, and acted upon what I saw in my imagination. The power of God hit her. She came back with a doctor's report stating that she was completely healed! The blood was completely transformed, both in her body and in the test tubes—there was no Hepatitis C. This testimony is on YouTube.

> *When anyone hears the word of the kingdom, and does not understand it, then the wicked one comes and snatches away what was sown in his heart. This is he who received seed by the wayside* (Matthew 13:19).

She was a bit fearful that the disease would come back. The enemy can come to snatch away the seed, but we prayed for this, too, and to this day she is completely healed.

Another time I was waiting upon the Lord and I had a supernatural encounter where I was caught up into the third heaven and I was seated at the Lord's Table. I have had encounters before where I have sat at the Lord's Table or seen the Lord in different forms. Once I was at the Table and I saw the Lord as a glorious King. He was a beautiful man. His eyes were blue and on His head He had a beautiful crown filled with incredible jewels. The crown came down on the sides, and His eyes were filled with such incredible love that they seemed to just go through me. He was a powerful and glorious King and not a gentle lamb. I've also had several encounters where I have just sat and ate with the Lord at His Table.

This particular night I was at the Table, and at the end of the Table I saw this incredible being. I thought it was either an archangel or a very powerful warrior angel. I knew (I didn't see) there was a company of angels—an army—behind him. I thought to myself, "Where is the Lord? Where is the Lord?"

His eyes were blue and on His head He had a beautiful crown filled with incredible jewels.

Putting this into human words, He said to me, "I am the Commander of the Lord's Hosts." I believe it was the same manifestation of the Lord who stood before Joshua with the drawn sword. It was the Lord as the Commander of the army; He was in a warrior form.

He spoke to me and said that there are many families who have darkness in their lives and are being tormented by the enemy, and there are many families who are going to have Satan's army leave their posts and flee. These families would be completely delivered that weekend at the meeting. I kept thinking, "Praise the Lord!"

On the Table were many weird items like cutlery and cups that I had never seen before. There was a vessel that looked like a gravy boat—it had a gold stem and was made out of diamonds—however it had wine in it. The Lord said that this was a wine of warfare. I knew that, as a wine of warfare, if drunk it would break strongholds and release joy never experienced before. When a person comes under the power of God and such joy overtakes his body, I believe strongholds are broken. Psalm 2 is about warfare, but He who sits in Heaven shall laugh (see Ps. 2:4).

> *And provide for those who grieve in Zion—to bestow on them a crown of beauty instead of ashes, the oil of joy instead of mourning* (Isaiah 61:3 NIV).

When a person comes under the power of God and such joy overtakes his body, I believe strongholds are broken.

The next day at Field of Dreams church I gave an alter call and I spoke about the encounter I had the previous evening. I said I was going to act out the drinking of this wine by faith and I knew that whoever partook in drinking it would be completely delivered from the oppression of the enemy. As I was doing this, people were falling down under the power of God and laughing. A woman named Deborah came up to me and was quite upset. She wanted her family to be delivered—her mother was in a coma and the doctors said there was no hope, so the family was preparing for the funeral. Deborah was beside herself because her mother was an atheist and she wanted her mother to be saved. As I touched her mouth I declared that her mother would be fine and that the power of darkness would be broken off the family. As she received this wine of warfare in the spirit, she felt as if a dark blindfold had fallen from her eyes and she fell down laughing. The next day she went to visit her mother. Her mother was sitting up in her hospital bed and said, "Hello Deborah!" as Deborah walked into the room. The medical staff was bewildered. Deborah's mother was led to the Lord that very day and she is a living testimony of God's miraculous healing power.

These testimonies back up what I am teaching. The following Scripture verses also further demonstrate the use of the imagination:

> *But his delight is in the law of the Lord, and in His law he meditates day and night. He shall be like a tree planted by the rivers of water, that brings forth its fruit in its season, whose leaf also shall not wither; and whatever he does shall prosper* (Psalm 1:2-3).

The word *law* means God's Word. Meditating is using the imagination. Those who delight in and meditate on the Word of the Lord day and night will prosper.

> *Then Jesus answered and said to them, "Most assuredly, I say to you, the Son can do nothing of Himself, but what He sees the Father do; for whatever He does, the Son also does in like manner"* (John 5:19).

Jesus *saw* Nathanael sitting under the fig tree in the spirit before He saw him in the natural:

> *Jesus answered and said to him, "Because I said to you, 'I saw you under the fig tree,' do you believe? You will see greater things than these"* (John 1:50).

> *Truly I tell you, if anyone says to this mountain, "Go, throw yourself into the sea," and does not doubt in their heart but believes that what they say will happen, it will be done for them. Therefore I tell you, whatever you ask for in prayer, believe that you have received it, and it will be yours* (Mark 11:23-24 NIV).

Again, I believe that the mind is referring to your imagination.

Jesus regularly went up to the mountain top and had encounters with His Father. I believe He was using His imagination and meditating on what the Father showed Him and wanted Him to do. Jesus carried that down from the mountain and released the Kingdom of Heaven into the natural. He also said, "Behold, the Kingdom of Heaven is upon you." Every miracle, sign, and wonder was manifested on earth because Jesus saw it happen in the spirit first.

In summary, this is how you activate your gifts and bring the supernatural into the natural: God shows you an image or a vision, you build it up in your imagination, and when you see the image and start believing it you activate your faith. Then you start to decree it, calling things as they are in Heaven, and then you step out and release it into the natural realm.

NOTES

1. Tony Cauchi, "Tommy Hicks," Voice of Healing, January 2012, accessed February 06, 2013, http://www.voiceofhealing.info/05otherministries/hicks.html.

2. Tony Cauchi, "Evan Roberts," Revival Library, November 2007, accessed February 06, 2013, http://www.revival-library.org/pensketches/revivalists/robertse.html.

chapter 9

Declare Victory by Faith

It is very important that when you make a decree, you decree out of the faith realm and not in human positive thinking. As I mentioned in the previous chapter, visualization is recalling your memory or resurrecting your past or current testimonies of your life and meditating on them. This builds your faith, and when you build your faith you increase your ability to create. People will often ask how they can build their faith to such a point where they can step out in boldness and make it a reality in their natural life.

I can confidently say that we all have had times in our lives where God has provided for us miraculously; otherwise, our Christianity would have died out by now. God is a faithful

God. This is how God has really helped me to build my faith—I always recall some of the miraculous situations in my past where God has helped me. A testimony helps us to overcome:

And they overcame him by the blood of the Lamb and by the word of their testimony, and they did not love their lives to the death (Revelation 12:11).

> *We all have had times in our lives where God has provided for us miraculously; otherwise, our Christianity would have died out by now.*

I often recall one particular supernatural moment which increases my faith, especially before I step out to do a meeting or evangelize. In the late 1980s to early 1990s, I was in a Christian rock band with my wife Paula. We had only been married for one year, and we used to travel with the other band members to perform at events including Youth Alive meetings around South Australia. One time we decided to have a break to refresh and we went camping a few hours away from town. It was a very cold and dark night, and we had our fire burning in a mini barbeque instead of on the ground. The flames were leaping out of this barbeque, and as we were talking about the Lord a man appeared out of nowhere. He was a tall, largely-built man with evil-looking eyes, and I sensed a demonic presence over him. He looked at us and walked over to where we were sitting and said to us, "I know who you people are!" I asked him who he was, and he replied that he was a Satanist and knew that we were Christians.

He started challenging us on spiritual things and we challenged him about God, and our conversation soon began to get heated. He was getting so angry that at one point he grabbed a spare camping chair and slammed it on the ground. He looked at me, as I was the leader of the group, and said to me, "I want you to pray for me. I'm going to sit in that chair and you can pray for me." Pointing to a band member he said, "If I don't have an encounter with God or become born again, I am going to punch you out." Then he pointed to another and said "I'm going to roundhouse kick you in the face." Then he pointed at me and said, "I'm going to tip that hot, burning barbecue on your head, burn your face off, and then I'm going to rape your wife!"

A dead silence permeated through the camp. In my head I was saying to him, "Mister, don't hold back now! Tell me what you are really thinking!" I asked him to give us a second so that I could talk to the band members. We stepped aside and I said to them, "Okay, this is where the rubber meets the road now. We need faith to step out and pray for this man. We either deny Christ or not." The man sat down and waved us over to come pray for him. We surrounded him and laid hands on him, and we started praying in tongues pleading the blood of Jesus. Within a couple of minutes this man started shaking, and then his shaking began to increase. He started crying and he covered his face with his hands before he fell to his knees; he was a quivering mess. Every demonic power which was in him left and he was completely delivered.

> *"Okay, this is where the rubber meets the road now. We need faith to step out and pray for this man. We either deny Christ or not."*

He received Christ as we led him through the sinner's prayer and he became born again. The whole countenance of his face changed; he was completely transformed, and there was a supernatural peace over him. Then the Holy Spirit released peace over the whole campsite. He went away to fetch his tent and came back to our site and even camped with us. There was no fear that night, only peace. The next day he thanked us for setting him free. We offered to disciple him and asked him to join us, but he declined, saying he knew of a church where he could fellowship. God is a faithful God!

Paul writes in Second Timothy, *"If we are faithless, He remains faithful; He cannot deny Himself"* (2 Tim. 2:13). Faith is like walking a plank—you step out and you can't see anything in the natural, but as soon as you get to the end of the plank God will always reveal Himself. You cannot activate faith by being fearful, discouraged, or disappointed. If you start decreeing out of your soulish realm, you have the potential to abort your mission. In Luke 1, Zacharias was chosen by lot to burn the incense inside the temple:

And the whole multitude of the people was praying outside at the hour of incense. Then an angel of the Lord appeared to him, standing on the right side of the altar of incense. And when Zacharias saw him, he was troubled, and fear fell upon him. But the angel said to him, "Do not be afraid, Zacharias, for your prayer is heard; and your wife Elizabeth will bear you a son, and you shall call his name John. And you will have joy and gladness, and many will rejoice at his birth. For he will be great in the sight of the Lord, and shall drink neither wine nor strong drink. He will also be filled with the Holy Spirit, even from his mother's womb. And he will turn many of the children of Israel to the Lord their God. He will also go before Him in the spirit and power of Elijah, 'to turn the hearts of the fathers to the children,' and the disobedient to the wisdom of the just, to make ready a people prepared for the Lord." And Zacharias said to the angel, "How shall I know this? For I am an old man, and my wife is well advanced in years." And the angel answered and said to him, "I am Gabriel, who stands in the presence of God, and was sent to speak to you and bring you these glad tidings.

But behold, you will be mute and not able to speak until the day these things take place, because you did not believe my words which will be fulfilled in their own time" (Luke 1:10-20).

Faith is like walking a plank—you step out and you can't see anything in the natural, but as soon as you get to the end of the plank God will always reveal Himself.

For years Zacharias had been praying for a son, and when God said it would be done, Zacharias doubted. I believe Zacharias came to a point of where he was just over it—over the praying, over the waiting. He had given up on believing that his prayer would be answered. It was disappointment and discouragement that came over Zacharias because his prayers had not been answered when he wanted them to be. Finally the promise came with the vision of the angel of the Lord, but he had "grumpy old man syndrome" and he challenged God with his unbelief. Zacharias's words of unbelief would have led to words of death which would have aborted the mission of John being born; therefore, the Lord had to shut his mouth.

We have to be careful not to speak out of fear, as this can create word curses and open doors to demonic powers in the heavenlies. We need to discipline our minds to meditate on the things above where Christ is seated. From my experience, this has empowered me to speak out as if I'm speaking the very words of God and seeing a manifestation of creative miracles.

> *We need to discipline our minds to meditate*
> *on the things above where Christ is seated.*

Here is another example of unbelief in the Scriptures:

Now there is in Jerusalem by the Sheep Gate a pool, which is called in Hebrew, Bethesda, having five porches. In these lay a great multitude of sick people, blind, lame, paralyzed, waiting for the moving of the water. For an angel went down at a certain time into the pool and stirred up the water; then whoever stepped in first, after the stirring of the water, was made well of whatever disease he had. Now a certain man was there who had an infirmity thirty-eight years. When Jesus saw him lying there, and knew that he already had been in that condition a long time, He said to him, "Do you want to be made well?" The sick man answered Him, "Sir, I have no man to put me into the pool when the water is stirred up; but while I am coming, another steps down before me." Jesus said to him, "Rise, take up your bed and walk." And immediately the man was made well, took up his bed, and walked (John 5:2-9).

There was an open heaven over the water—the angels were ascending and descending from Heaven. Jesus saw unbelief over the sick man. This man had been in doubt, and he was discouraged and disappointed because he had been in this condition for thirty-eight years. When Jesus asked him if he wanted to get well he replied with a whining demeanor, but Jesus had compassion for him and supernaturally released healing through His spoken word. This man was not in a place to receive healing himself as he had no faith. We have the ability to rise up and activate the faith realm, but Jesus can sovereignly heal somebody who is in unbelief. The Lord can move over people and heal those who do not have faith.

I remember watching a video of a Kathryn Kuhlman meeting in 1975 where God sovereignly healed an atheist scientist who was totally deaf in one ear. His ear popped open and Kathryn asked him if he now believed in God and he replied that yes, now he believed. God does not require people to first be saved before they can be healed; God can heal the unbeliever and the faithless as a sign and wonder in order for people to become born again. God has compassion over people, and He will move over them with His sovereignty.

Christians new to the faith need to be guided or "mothered" so to speak; they are like babies who need to be fed and have their diapers changed. I would not be happy to still be changing my son's diaper now that he is twenty. In the same way, Christians need to grow and mature and expand their faith. We move on from the elementary teachings of Christ, and we go into the maturity of eating solid food. God wants us to exercise our senses and come into a place of dominion where we start to self-govern our own lives with faith, to walk as Jesus walked. He wants us to have victory and bear fruit, and once we can self-govern then we can govern the Kingdom of Heaven here on earth. He wants us to walk in a faith realm where we are mature enough to bring the miraculous to earth without having to wait for God to sovereignly do it, for we need to be the governors here on earth. *"He who says he abides in Him ought himself also to walk just as He walked"* (1 John 2:6). We need to walk as Jesus walked. Once we start to see and activate the supernatural seed by operating in the realm of God, we start to decree God's will and move as He intended for us to operate here on earth.

> *God does not require people to first be saved before they can be healed; God can heal the unbeliever and the faithless as a sign and wonder in order for people to become born again.*

Todd Weatherly and I have seen many miracles and experienced many amazing encounters. This is a testimony of how God miraculously turned a horrible situation around for His glory: Todd and I were on the island of Negros in the Philippines. One day we had 400 to 500 decisions for Christ from both adults and children who were partaking in one of our feeding programs, and it was such an awesome day. In the evening we held a pastors' conference, and I was preaching. In the middle of the preaching, Todd came up to me and interrupted the meeting. I was concerned as Todd had never done anything like that before. Todd pulled me aside and quietly told me that there were 40 children from the morning's feeding program in the hospital with food poisoning. In the Philippines they have minimal facilities for dealing with sicknesses and we were now in a very serious situation.

Todd had gone to the kitchen during the meeting as I was preaching and saw the main pastor for that island quite stressed out and beside himself. The Filipinos are usually very calm people, so this pastor's demeanor had caused Todd great concern. The pastor told Todd about the children being sick; he was so worried about them, but he was worried about his reputation being ruined, too. The cooks from that day were in a separate room and they were actually screaming and freaking out because of what had happened. Todd knew this situation was serious, so he decided to stop me in the middle of my preaching to tell me what had happened.

We did not panic; we could easily have "lost our cool," but instead we got into a faith realm and knew that our only hope was to trust in God. We started to meditate on the promises of God. We gathered the whole congregation of pastors and we all started to pray and call upon the Holy Spirit to baptize those pastors who needed to be baptized. We had an upper-room encounter, and the power of the Holy Spirit came upon us. God shook the place and we started prophesying into the situation for a good 45 minutes. The police were waiting outside the building ready to arrest us for poisoning the children, but they never entered the building. At one point, we felt as if we had a major breakthrough in the spirit realm and we decided to go to the hospital to pray for the children.

The police agreed to escort us to the hospital, and as we got closer to the town center where the hospital was located we saw a crowd of hundreds of people gathered. I asked the pastor who was driving us if there was a convention on in the city because of the crowd size, but the pastor said no. These people were actually the children's parents. The enemy had upped the stakes, and the situation was far worse than what we were originally told. There were 207 children in the hospital with food poisoning, and most of them were near death.

> *We had an upper-room encounter, and the power of the Holy Spirit came upon us. God shook the place and we started prophesying into the situation for a good 45 minutes.*

We could have been like Zacharias and become disappointed. We could have gone into unbelief, and worse yet we could have spiraled down with fear and it would have been the end of us. It did cross my mind that we might be killed—there was an angry mob with guns, clubs, and sticks waiting for us. The army had to be called in to control the crowd. Todd said to me, "Adam, I am right behind you. You can go first!" We got out of the car and I said to the crowd that they could do anything they wanted to do to us, but first we would like to pray for the children. Again, we thought we were either going to be beaten or killed or thrown into prison for the rest of our lives, but we knew we had to stay in that faith realm and rely totally on God.

It was so intense—there was pandemonium inside the hospital and the parents were angry and upset. There were rows of children lying down with their eyes rolled back until you could see the whites. There were children projectile-vomiting everywhere. The hospital was so full that some children were lying outside in rows on the footpath. We started praying and laying hands on the children throughout the night.

After a while, we felt something had changed in the spirit and the glory of God broke out in that hospital. Parents were frantically grabbing our hands, trying to put them on their own children's heads because as we were laying hands on them they were being completely healed. They would sit straight up and return to a picture of health. The hospital had gone from pandemonium and panic to excitement. As we continued praying, the children were being released from the hospital. About 2:30 AM, we were exhausted from physically laying hands on the children, but to God's glory He cleaned out that hospital!

As we left the hospital there was a lineup of children waiting to be released.

> *The hospital had gone from pandemonium*
> *and panic to excitement.*

We slept in the next day, and as we woke up we heard on the radio that the event had made national news. The mayor of the city summoned us, and we had the opportunity to sit in his office and share the gospel with him. After we left Negros and returned to Australia, we received an email a week later telling us that a revival had broken out in that city. The church was packed with standing room only. The parents of the children were so blessed and excited by what God had done that they came to the Lord. God had turned a disastrous situation into a miraculous healing and revival for His glory.

In Second Kings 13 is a passage of Scripture I want to use as an example of decreeing the Word of God through faith out of the revelatory realm. The king of Israel was in a really bad place and Israel was on the eve of destruction—she had sinned and was about to be destroyed, with the Syrian army breathing down her neck. Joash sought Elisha the prophet, but when he found Elisha he found a man on his deathbed. Joash wept and cried, *"O my father, my father, the chariots of Israel and their horsemen!"* (2 Kings 13:14). The prophet of the nation is dying at a time when he was most needed. Elisha told him to get a bow and some arrows. I can just imagine Joash thinking to himself that this was not the time to be getting a bow and arrow—all he really needed was a word from the Lord. I believe that Elisha saw something in the spirit but was too ill to act it out and that is why he sent Joash to get the bow and arrows. In acting out what Elisha saw, a paradigm was created to decree the Word of God.

> *Then he said to the king of Israel, "Put your hand on the bow." So he put his hand on it, and Elisha put his hands on the king's hands. And he said, "Open the east window"; and he opened it. Then Elisha said, "Shoot"; and he shot. And he said, "The arrow of the Lord's deliverance and the arrow of deliverance from Syria; for you must strike the Syrians at Aphek till you have destroyed them"* (2 Kings 13:16-17).

Joash must have thought Elisha was delirious. He himself was most probably not in a good place to take on board what Elisha was saying, because he took these arrows of victory and only struck the ground three times. Elisha rebuked Joash and was angry with him, saying he should have struck at least five or six times to secure the victory. Joash acted out of despair, not out of revelation.

There is a parable here in this passage of Scripture that God has shown me, and I use this to decree out of the heavenlies and bring it to earth. In the spirit, there are metaphors found in dreams and visions and Jesus speaks to us in parables. This passage of Scripture is a blueprint of how we should pray when there is a time of discouragement. A house can be a metaphor for the temple of the Holy Spirit in the New Covenant. A window is a metaphor for your eyes; the east window is the right side of the building which is metaphorically your right eye, which is the spiritual eye. "Open the window" is a parable of revelation and means to open your spiritual eye. Arrows symbolize words. When you open your spiritual eyes to the revelation of who we are in Christ, seated in heavenly places, and you begin prophesying against the enemy using your "victory arrows" or prophetic words, you will start to see a shift in the spirit realm. Elisha told the king to strike the ground—when you receive revelation, you hit the ground with passion and not with despair.

> *In the spirit, there are metaphors found in dreams and visions and Jesus speaks to us in parables.*

The revelation of our authority and our identity in Christ—that we are seated with Him in heavenly places and the same Spirit who raised Him from the dead is inside us— allows us to prophesy with the Lord's victory arrows against the enemy. This is when the miraculous will occur. The action of lifting your hand to strike the arrow into the ground means that you are taking the words from Heaven and releasing them here on earth. As it is in Heaven, so it will be on earth. You are releasing God's words into the natural Adamic realm. In the name of Jesus, we should be striking the ground and breaking off the curses over ourselves, our families, and our community. We need to prophesy revival into our cities, and we need to prophesy victory arrows over sickness and break the plans of the enemy. Use this blueprint to bring victory into your life and see how it will impact your community.

chapter 10

CITIZENS OF HEAVEN

THIS BOOK HAS MANY TESTIMONIES TO ENCOURAGE YOU. I won't say I am a very educated man—I was a high school dropout and I had dyslexia as a child. I am just an average person like all the other average people in the world, but God has transformed my life. I am still a work in progress and by faith every day I put on the armor of God; I prophesy into my mind that I am possessed by the revelation and the image of God and that the pathways of my mind are streamlined into the revelation of Jesus Christ. I prophesy to my brain that it is sanctified, limitless, and operates at 100 percent. I can even testify to a time when a woman who had seen me preach over several years came up to me and said, "Something has happened to you, sir." She went on to tell me that my vocabulary had changed and that it was as if my brain had expanded. Initially I found this insulting, but the Lord rebuked me because I had been praying for my brain to expand for years. This was a testimony to show that God had been expanding my brain and my mind with the revelation of who He is.

> *I prophesy into my mind that I am possessed*
> *by the revelation and the image of God and*
> *that the pathways of my mind are streamlined*
> *into the revelation of Jesus Christ.*

I want to encourage every believer in Christ that God can use you, He can empower you with His glory, and He can shine through you. I believe there is a generation rising up that will perform many signs, wonders, and miracles like we have never seen before. The Bible says that when two or more are gathered in His name, Christ will be among them (see Matt. 18:20). When you pray and agree with God's Word, the Holy Spirit agrees with you. He is within you and He intercedes on your behalf. When some people pray, they pray out of the citizenship of their country and their soul. It is one thing to pray out of your soulish desires, begging God to answer you, but it is a far more effective experience to pray out of your citizenship of Heaven. If you start agreeing with the Holy Spirit, praying the promises of God, and praying out of your citizenship of Heaven, you and the Holy Spirit are already two agreeing in the spirit. If you are praying with the Holy Spirit and someone else, a third party joins you in prayer and agrees with you. The Word says that God will honor that prayer.

> *Again I say unto you, That if two of you shall agree on earth as touching any thing that they shall ask, it shall be done for them of my Father which is in heaven. For where two or three are gathered together in my name, there am I in the midst of them* (Matthew 18:19-20 KJV).

When your vocabulary lines up with the Word of God and the promises of Heaven, the answers to your prayers will be fast-tracked. Just wait—you will start to see and experience the miraculous.

Through doing this I have gone from being a carnal man who went to church on a Sunday just to religiously pay homage to God to actually being totally transformed into a supernatural man, walking the way Jesus walked. God spoke to me several years ago about how the things of the world are going to change, and I see it happening.

I want to use this analogy from the book of Genesis. Abraham and Lot came to a place of not "getting on well"—they didn't see eye to eye, and when they came out of Egypt they had to separate. I believe that God is not into separating the church permanently. There is a divine appointment where God is removing "Lot" from the body of Christ. He is removing the carnal Christian and allowing a sanctified separation to occur.

The carnal Christian is metaphorically going into the world, just like in the days of Sodom. They are being seduced by the world and have compromised their ways and become dependent on the ways of the world and its provision.

> *I have gone from being a carnal man who went to church on a Sunday just to religiously pay homage to God to actually being totally transformed into a supernatural man, walking the way Jesus walked.*

Abraham was separated from Lot to come into the promise of Isaac. Isaac can symbolize the promise of revival. I believe in these last days God is raising up His Bride as a corporate spirit of Elijah. This corporate body is becoming a supernatural entity of men and women who have been made spotless in His righteousness. There will be no elite denominations or brick and mortar—only supernatural people who are corporately ushering in an end-times massive revival which will ultimately usher in the Bridegroom, Jesus Christ. This is currently happening. The enemy will very soon be found in a fetal position sucking his thumb when the body of Christ rises up and walks into their supernatural destiny.

I encourage you to rise up and cultivate the Kingdom of God in this hour.

If you feel this book has challenged you in your Christian

walk, below is a prayer you can pray with me.

Heavenly Father, I repent of serving You half-heartedly. Lord Jesus, I pledge my allegiance with You, and I thank You for saving me through Your obedience to the cross of Calvary. I confess with my mouth that Jesus is Lord and I believe that You, Father, raised Jesus from the dead. Thank You for empowering me with the baptism of Your Spirit. I believe that now I am a living testimony of First John 2:6. Walking the way Jesus walked as a supernatural man, I give You the glory by ushering the Kingdom of God onto the earth with like-minded believers, preparing the Bride of Christ for His second coming. In Jesus name, amen.

TESTIMONIES

In 2010 I had a number of strokes. I was told I had two big ones and two small ones. I was fighting for my life from February to October of that year and needed twelve months of intense physiotherapy to learn to walk again. I was also diagnosed at that time with two conditions of the brain, both life threatening and incurable. Both conditions were limiting my ability to move at times and live a normal life. Regular MRIs of my brain were done at the same hospital, allowing my neurology specialists to monitor my condition. I had an MRI in May of last year (2012) which again showed that over half of the arteries and blood vessels in my brain were closed, which meant I could have had another stroke at any time. When I asked my specialist if there was anything else they could do to open the arteries or the veins of my brain he said "we have done all we can, there is no cure." He had never said this to me before. So I said to the Lord, "I'm relying totally on You to heal me, to open up my veins and arteries so I may live, for Your Glory." Hope City Church had Adam F. Thompson ministering for a weekend in August 2012. Adam called me out to the front and spoke a word of knowledge over me. He said that the Lord wanted to bring healing to my brain. Adam didn't know me or anything about me including my brain, but Jesus did. I claimed and thanked Jesus for this healing and my health started to improve. I was now able to go for long walks of thirty to sixty minutes at a time, something that was previously impossible.

Last December (2012) I needed to have another MRI. The three neurologists were excited when they gave me the results. The MRI showed that all the arteries and veins in my brain had opened up. I asked for a printout of the MRI and I said to one of the specialists, "Doctor, this looks like a miracle." To this he replied, "I think so." One of the doctors wrote on the back of the test results of the remarkable improvement to my brain. Jesus has healed me of a rare and incurable condition of the brain which could have killed me at any moment. Praise His Holy Name. I also thank Jesus for His obedient servant, Adam, for bringing His Kingdom healing on earth for me as it is in Heaven.

Carmel Risson
Melbourne, Victoria. Australia

DOCTOR'S NOTES

The patency of the vessels
have remarkebly improved
from previous 2 MRIs
And this should translate
into better blood perfusion
to the brain cells.

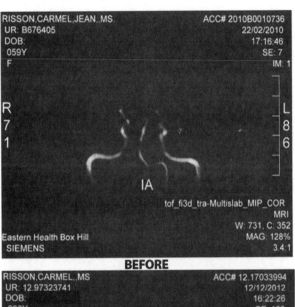

BEFORE

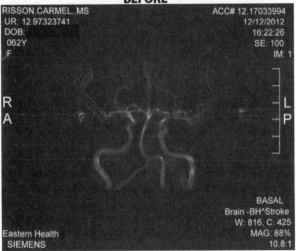

AFTER

In the BEFORE scan you will be able to see the pressure build up in the brain.
In the AFTER scan you will be able to see no pressure build up in the brain and
no signs of stroke with normal blood flow. PRAISE GOD.

Dear Adam,

Two prophetic words you spoke over my ten-year-old daughter came to pass! You said "God will give your daughter new, healthy friendships." Her best friend of several years watches R-rated movies and *Twilight*. We have been concerned about this and have told her the importance of having friends with the same values. Tonight, my daughter said she had made a *new* best friend who does not watch those movies or shows.

You also said, "Everything will work out with her teacher." (We had a difficult issue with her teacher earlier in the year.) At graduation, her teacher awarded my daughter two of the highest trophies that a student can get for having the highest GPA and the best character.

We praise God for you, Adam. Your prophetic gift is accurate. We had never met you before and you spoke into situations in our daughter's life that were very important to us. Thank you for seeking God and allowing His river to flow out of you to bless others.

SUSIE
Raleigh, North Carolina, USA

Last January (2012) our sons and their wives were at a Field of Dreams Church service. You called them out and gave them words. One of the things you told our eldest son and his wife was, "You will have not only a child, but children." Two weeks later, she was having female problems and was told by doctors that she had endometriosis and only one of her ovaries was functioning, so she may not be able to get pregnant. Remembering the word given by you two weeks earlier, they decided to believe God. A short while ago they decided to start a family, and she got pregnant very easily and last Saturday was 13 weeks pregnant! God is awesome.

JUDE PFEIFFER
South Australia
Attends Field of Dreams Church

I was having trouble with my eyes and was diagnosed with glaucoma. I have been having treatment for about two years. In December 2010, the specialist told me the pressure in my eye was rising, which was not a good sign. Also the eye felt like it had sand in it all the time and I was always blinking, trying to clear it. In February this year (2011), during church Adam had a word of knowledge that someone was having trouble with the right eye and I jumped up straight away and went forward for prayer. Adam spoke to the condition and I felt something change in that eye so that it was no longer uncomfortable. I said, "I can see better now and it's more comfortable." Adam told me to turn around to the congregation and tell the people, and I did with a thankful heart. Two weeks later I was scheduled for more tests at the specialist and the results proved to be excellent and showed the eye pressure had returned to normal. The specialist thinks the treatment arrested the glaucoma, but I praise the Lord my sight is improved and my eyes are comfortable. Jesus did it. Of course!

JAMES POOLEY
South Australia
Attends Field of Dreams Church

A few months ago (June 2012) I was at the Soaker Service at Field of Dreams when Adam gave me a word of knowledge that he was seeing a young man walking through a door. He asked me if I had any children and I replied yes, two adult boys. I then said I believe it is my eldest son walking into the Kingdom of God. He then asked the church to all pray for my son.

I kept on praying for my two sons' salvation and then two weeks ago (November 2012) my eldest son gave his life to the Lord! *Praise the Lord!* And thank you, Adam, for being obedient to our Father.

AMANDA FORD
South Australia

I spoke at our meeting yesterday. As I was preparing, I remembered your meetings here in Canberra—how you moved with words of knowledge. I've never moved in that before, but remembering how you did your meetings, the day before I spoke I asked the Lord for words of knowledge for the meeting. The Lord gave me nine specific words of knowledge for different people and seven responded to those words—amazing, God! Thank you for coming to Canberra; your ministry encouraged me to move out more in the supernatural. God bless you continually with uncommon blessings!

NOA MURANYI
Canberra, Australia

I had been having problems with my digestive system for over 20 years. I would double over and sometimes faint from the pain. There were times that I would wake up in the middle of the night covered in sweat, heart pounding, short of breath, and scared. Paramedics could not find the problem. I thought my problem was irritable bowel syndrome. When I had gone for allergy tests the first time, the doctor said I had no food allergies and still I was getting very bad pain in my stomach and bowels. I went for tests again seven years ago and was tested allergic to potatoes, tomatoes, green and wax beans, chicken, beef, pork, yeast, apples, and peanuts. On the second day of the Cloverdale Church Conference in Vancouver, as I waited to share my dream with Adam, he stopped mid-prayer over my friend Alex and said that there was someone who had peanut allergies. I responded, "I'm right here." As Adam prayed I felt something inside me flicker, and I knew right away that God healed me of allergies. I did not wait to test it. I ate that night. God healed all the allergies I had. No pain or embarrassing effects. I ate an apple this morning! Praise God! Thanks, Adam.

TAMMY MACKIE
Vancouver, Canada

Hi, Adam,

You had a prophetic word over a lady who was in her late 60s and you spoke about money coming to her. She has never won anything in her life. Two days after the meeting she won 5,000 dollars at a shopping center. She was amazed. Thanks for coming and blessing us.

ANDREW MAGRATH
Hope City Church
Victoria, Australia

Hey Adam,

At the Field of Dreams Soaker Service you called out a word of knowledge about someone whose mom had passed away and there was a piece of her jewelry missing. Well, I went forward for that because a very unique brooch of my mom's had gone missing. I was talking to my dad about it on Saturday, saying that we had checked all her clothes, handbags, jewelry boxes, etc., and it was nowhere to be found. Guess what? Today it is in her jewelry box along with all her other jewelry! Praise God, He is so good to us! Thanks, Adam.

Libby Cunningham
South Australia
Attends Field of Dreams Church

I am overjoyed to be able to report a wonderful miracle, and an answer to many prayers. About five or six months ago I was at the Field of Dreams soaker service. As Adam was ministering, I heard him call out that God had given him a word of knowledge concerning a woman named Madeleine. I immediately thought of our Maddie, but she wasn't there. Then Adam said, "She may be the daughter of someone who is present here tonight." I went out the front to receive the word for her, and Adam asked me if she had lost any babies through miscarriage and if there was something wrong with her womb. I replied 'Yes' to both questions, and told him she had advanced endometriosis. Adam prayed for her womb to be healed. I could feel faith being released. Then he prophesied and called forth a child. It was powerful. He looked at me and said something like, "Don't worry, it's ok. She'll have a baby soon." I believed him. I phoned Maddie the next day and she received the word with such happiness, I did a little dance! I am delighted to tell you that at the writing of this testimony, Madeleine and Daniel are expecting a baby! She is 14 weeks, and all is well! To Your Name be all the praise Lord Jesus! Amen!

PELITA WEBB
South Australia
9 Feb 2013

ABOUT
ADAM F. THOMPSON

Adam F. Thompson is the co-author of *The Divinity Code to Understanding Your Dreams and Visions*. He has a remarkable grace to interpret dreams, move in words of knowledge, and demonstrate the prophetic. Supernatural signs and manifestations regularly accompany his ministry as he desires to see Jesus magnified through the moving of the Holy Spirit. He has ministered extensively in the USA, Canada, Australia, New Zealand, China, Hong Kong, Pakistan, India, Africa, Indonesia, New Guinea, Malaysia, and the Philippines in crusades, feeding programs, and pastors' conferences. Adam has also been instrumental in planting Field of Dreams Church in South Australia.